D1543668

Just for Kids
BIBLE

FAVORITE READINGS
FOR ACTIVE KIDS
NEW
INTERNATIONAL
VERSION

Chariot Books
David C. Cook Publishing Co.

Published by Chariot Books™,
an imprint of David C. Cook Publishing Co.
David C. Cook Publishing Co., Elgin, Illinois 60120
David C. Cook Publishing Co., Weston, Ontario
Nova Distribution Ltd., Torquay, England

JUST-FOR-KIDS BIBLE
© 1989, 1990, 1991 by David C. Cook Publishing Co.

Illustrated by Richard Williams
Edited by Lori Frankis
Internal design by Nancy L. Haskins
Cover design by Koechel Peterson and Associates, Inc.

All rights reserved. Except for brief excerpts for review purposes, no part of this book
may be reproduced or used in any form without written permission from the publisher.

Scripture is taken from the *Holy Bible, New International Version,* © 1973, 1978, 1984,
International Bible Society. Used by permission of Zondervan Bible Publishers

First Printing, 1991
Printed in the United States of America
95 94 93 92 91   5 4 3 2 1

Library of Congress Cataloging in Publication Data
Just-For-Kids Bible
p. cm.
Summary: Favorite Bible stories from Creation to the apostles, accompanied by
introductions, character traits, and verses to memorize.
ISBN 1-55513-713-X
1. Bible stories, English. [1. Bible stories.] I. Chariot books.
BS551.2.J875 1991
220.9'505—dc20
                                                            91-17565
                                                              CIP
                                                              AC

Black
Sea

GALATIA

To: _Tara_

From: _Daddy & Denise_

CYPRUS

Mediterranean
Sea

Character traits have been taken from
The Illustrated Bible, Living Values Edition.
©1989 David C. Cook Publishing Co.

Most Bible memory verses coordinate with the Bible-in-Life
junior age curriculum from David C. Cook Publishing Co.

Thanks to the team that made this book possible:
Cathy Davis, April Frost, Dawn Lauck, Randy Maid, Paul Mouw, Brian Reck, Julie Smith

At last,
A Bible you can read
...and understand.
Psst! Want to know a secret?

A lot of people (even some grown-ups) think the Bible is hard to read and even harder to understand. Well, it doesn't have to be. Here's what we've done to make this Bible one you'll understand.

1 In *The Just-for-Kids Bible* each story is told in just a couple of pages. We've selected the verses from the Bible that give you the heart of the story. All the Bible readings look like this:

📖 **By day the LORD went ahead of them in a pillar of cloud to guide them on their way and by night in a pillar of fire to give them light, so that they could travel by day or night. Neither the pillar of cloud by day nor the pillar of fire by night left its place in front of the people.**

2 Then we've added some information that tells you a little about what you're reading, what came before, or what comes next. These comments look like this:

God had chosen Moses to deliver his people, Israel, from Pharaoh in Egypt. When all the firstborn Egyptian children died one night, Pharaoh agreed to let Israel go. God led Israel around by the desert road toward the Red Sea.

3 Another way to remember what God is teaching you is to memorize a Bible verse that talks about a key idea from the story. God will use the verses you memorize now to help and encourage you throughout life.

■ Memory Verse:
Hebrews 11:1
Now faith is being sure of what we hope for and certain of what we do not see.

5. Plus there's a picture to look at. It's always more fun to read a story when there's a picture along with it. You can imagine what it would have been like to have lived in Bible times.

4 The Character Trait is a key idea you can apply to your life. Sometimes the person in the Bible story is a good example of someone who has this trait in his or her life. Other times, you'll read about people who didn't have the trait, and the problems that caused. These character traits can be building blocks for your life, to help you love God and live for Him every day.

■ Character Trait:

Confidence—a feeling of security based on faith and trust. It is the belief that God will take care of you in any situation—no matter what the circumstances. Moses had confidence in God's ability to deliver Israel from the Egyptians.

Now that you know what's in this book, give it a try. Reading one story a day, or even one story a week, is a good way to start. Some kids like to read their Bible first thing in the morning, and others like to read it just before they go to sleep. Find a time that's good for your schedule, when you won't be interrupted or in a hurry. Pretty soon, you'll discover that reading your Bible has become a habit you enjoy—just like an after-school snack! And best of all, you'll start finding you have the courage of Daniel or the confidence of Moses as you grow in your walk with God.

TABLE OF CONTENTS

New
Testament

Old Testament

■ Genesis 1:3-5, 7, 8, 12, 13, 17, 28-31, 18, 21-23,

In the Beginning

Before God created the world everything was dark and silent. Then He made heaven and earth. His Spirit moved through the darkness and across the waters.

📖 **And God said, "Let there be light," and there was light. God saw that the light was good, and he separated the light from the darkness. God called the light "day," and the darkness he called "night." And there was evening, and there was morning—the first day.**

On the second day, God made the sky and water.

📖 **So God made the expanse and separated the water under the expanse from the water above it. And it was so.**

● ●

■ Memory Verse:

Psalm 19:1
The heavens declare the glory of God; the skies proclaim the work of his hands.

■ Character Trait:

Purposefulness—The determination to complete whatever you set out to do. When God gives someone a job to do, that person should feel a sense of purpose as he or she tries to do what God has said to do.

God called the expanse "sky." **And there was evening, and there was morning—the second day.**

On the third day, God gathered the waters under the sky. He called these "seas." He named the dry land "earth." On the land He made grass and flowers and trees, and in each was the seed to make another one exactly like the first one.

📖 **The land produced vegetation: plants bearing seed according to their kinds and trees bearing fruit with seed in it according to their kinds. And God saw that it was good. And there was evening, and there was morning—the third day.**

On the fourth day, God made the sun, moon, and stars. The days, years, and seasons were also set by God.

📖 **God set them in the expanse of the sky to give light on the earth, to govern the day and the night, and to separate light from darkness.**

And God saw that it was good.

On the fifth day God made fish and birds.

📖 So God created the great creatures of the sea and every living and moving thing with which the water teems, according to their kinds, and every winged bird according to its kind. And God saw that it was good. God blessed them and said, "Be fruitful and increase in number and fill the water in the seas, and let the birds increase on the earth." And there was evening, and there was morning—the fifth day.

On the sixth day God created animals and the first man, Adam. He was the greatest of all God's creations, for God gave him a mind to choose between good and evil, and a soul that would live forever.

📖 God blessed them and said to them, "Be fruitful and increase in number;

fill the earth and subdue it. Rule over the fish of the sea and the birds of the air and over every living creature that moves on the ground."

Then God said, "I give you every seed-bearing plant on the face of the whole earth and every tree that has fruit with seed in it. They will be yours for food. And to all the beasts of the earth and all the birds of the air and all the creatures that move on the ground—everything that has the breath of life in it— I give every green plant for food." And it was so. God saw all that he had made, and it was very good. And there was evening, and there was morning—the sixth day.

Man: The Crown of God's Creation

God placed Adam in a beautiful garden in the east, in Eden. In the middle of the garden He placed the tree of life and the tree of the knowledge of good and evil.

📖 The LORD God took the man and put him in the Garden of Eden to work it and take care of it. And the LORD God commanded the man, "You are free to eat from any tree in the garden; but you must not eat from the Tree of the Knowledge of Good and Evil, for when you eat of it you will surely die."

The LORD God said, "It is not good for the man to be alone. I will make a helper suitable for him.

So the LORD God caused the man to fall into a deep sleep; and while he was sleeping, he took one of the man's ribs and closed up the place with flesh. Then the LORD God made a woman from the rib he had taken out of the man, and he brought her to the man.

The man said, "This is now bone of my bones and flesh of my flesh; she shall be called 'woman,' for she was taken out of man."

For this reason a man will leave his father and mother and be united to his wife, and they will become one flesh.

■ **Memory Verse:**

Genesis 1:26

Then God said, "Let us make man in our image, in our likeness, and let them rule over the fish of the sea and the birds of the air, over the livestock, over all the earth, and over all the creatures that move along the ground."

■ **Character Trait:**

Fellowship—when two or more people who have similar interests have feelings of friendship between them. Christians are able to experience fellowship in a special way, because their common interest is Jesus.

■ Genesis 3:4, 5, 7, 11-13, 23, 24

God Gives a Choice

The serpent was the sneakiest of all the creatures God had made. He knew that God had given Adam and Eve everything in the garden except for the tree of the knowledge of good and evil. So he tempted Eve.

📖 **"You will not surely die," the serpent said to the woman. "For God knows that when you eat of it your eyes will be opened, and you will be like God, knowing good and evil."**

So Eve ate the fruit and gave some to Adam. He ate it, too.

■ **Memory Verse:**
Romans 3:23
For all have sinned and fall short of the glory of God.

■ **Character Trait:**
Obedience—doing what you are told to do. We are commanded to be obedient to God in every way. Obedience is part of our faith because it shows we know that God can teach us and protect us.

📖 And he said, "Who told you that you were naked? Have you eaten from the tree that I commanded you not to eat from?" The man said, "The woman you put here with me—she gave me some fruit from the tree, and I ate it." Then the LORD God said to the woman, "What is this you have done? . . ."

So the LORD God banished him from the Garden of Eden to work the ground from which he had been taken. After he drove the man out, he placed on the east side of the Garden of Eden cherubim and a flaming sword flashing back and forth to guard the way to the tree of life.

📖 Then the eyes of both of them were opened, and they realized they were naked; so they sewed fig leaves together and made coverings for themselves.

At once, Adam and Eve knew they had sinned against God and hid from Him. But God found them.

The First Murder

Adam and Eve had two children, Cain and Abel. Abel was a shepherd, and Cain was a farmer. For their offering to the Lord, Abel brought a lamb from his flock, and Cain brought fruits and vegetables from the soil.

📖 But on Cain and his offering he did not look with favor. So Cain was very angry, and his face was downcast. Then the Lord said to Cain, "Why are you angry? Why is your face downcast?"

God told Cain that if he would obey and bring the right kind of offering, it would be accepted. This made Cain angry and jealous of Abel.

📖 Now Cain said to his brother Abel, "Let's go out to the field."

And while they were in the field, Cain attacked his brother Abel and killed him.

Then the Lord said to Cain, "Where is your brother Abel?"

"I don't know," he replied. "Am I my brother's keeper?"

The Lord said, "What have you done? Listen! Your brother's blood cries out to me from the ground. Now you are under a curse and driven from the ground, which opened its mouth to receive your brother's blood from your hand. When you work the ground, it will no longer yield its crops for you. You will be a restless wanderer on the earth."

Cain said to the Lord, "My punishment is more than I can bear. Today you are driving me from the land,

and I will be hidden from your presence; I will be a restless wanderer on the earth, and whoever finds me will kill me."

But the Lᴏʀᴅ said to him, "Not so; if anyone kills Cain, he will suffer vengeance seven times over." Then the Lᴏʀᴅ put a mark on Cain so that no one who found him would kill him. So Cain went out from the Lᴏʀᴅ's presence and lived in the land of Nod, east of Eden.

■ Memory Verse:

Proverbs 3:12
Because the Lord disciplines those he loves, as a father the son he delights in.

■ Character Trait:

Obedience—promptly doing what you are told to do. The Bible tells us that we are to obey God always, no matter what the circumstances are.

Afloat in a Boat

Man's sin increased. Only Noah remained true to God. One day God told Noah that He would destroy the earth.

📖 So God said to Noah, "I am going to put an end to all people, for the earth is filled with violence because of them. I am surely going to destroy both them and the earth. So make yourself an ark of cypress wood; make rooms in it and coat it with pitch inside and out...

"I am going to bring floodwaters on the earth to destroy all life under the heavens, every creature that has the breath of life in it. Everything on earth will perish. But I will establish my covenant with you, and you will enter the ark—you and your sons and your wife and your sons' wives with you. You are to bring into the ark two of all living creatures, male and female, to keep them alive with you.Two of every kind of bird, of every kind of animal and of every kind of creature that moves along the ground will come to you to be kept alive. You are to take every kind of food that is to be eaten and store it away as food for you and for them."

When the ark was completed, God told Noah and his family to enter the ark, and to take with them seven pairs of each kind of animal and bird good to eat, and one pair of each kind not used for food.

📖 In the six hundredth year of Noah's life, on the seventeenth day of the second month—on that day all the springs of the great deep burst forth, and the floodgates of the heavens were opened. And rain fell on the earth forty days and forty nights.

Every living thing that moved on the earth perished—birds, livestock, wild animals, all the creatures that swarm over the earth, and all mankind. Everything on dry land that had the breath of life in its nostrils died. Every living thing on the face of the earth was wiped out; men and animals and the creatures that move along the ground and the birds of the air were wiped from the earth. Only Noah was left, and those with him in the ark. The waters flooded the earth for a hundred and fifty days.

At last the rain stopped and the ark rested on Mt. Ararat. Noah sent out a dove three times to see if the land was dry. When the dove didn't return the third time, Noah knew it had found a place to nest.

Then God said to Noah, "Come out of the ark, you and your wife and your sons and their wives... Bring out every kind of living creature that is with you—the birds, the animals, and all the creatures that move along the ground—so they can multiply on the earth and be fruitful and increase in number upon it."

"I have set my rainbow in the clouds, and it will be the sign of the covenant between me and the earth. Whenever I bring clouds over the earth and the rainbow appears in the clouds, I will remember my covenant between me and you and all living creatures of every kind. Never again will the waters become a flood to destroy all life.

Whenever the rainbow appears in the clouds, I will see it and remember the everlasting covenant between God and all living creatures of every kind on the earth."

■ Memory Verse:

Psalm 145:17
The Lord is righteous in all his ways and loving toward all he has made.

■ Character Trait:

Obedience—doing what you are told to do. We are commanded to obey God always. Obedience is part of our faith because it shows we know God can teach us and protect us, no matter what the circumstances.

Lot's Load of Trouble

The Lord warned Abraham that He was going to destroy Sodom and Gomorrah. But Abraham, knowing that Lot, his nephew, lived in Sodom, pleaded for God to have mercy on the city.

📖 **Then Abraham approached him and said: "Will you sweep away the righteous with the wicked? What if there are fifty righteous people in the city? Will you really sweep it away and not spare the place for the**

sake of the fifty righteous people in it? Far be it from you to do such a thing—to kill the righteous with the wicked, treating the righteous and the wicked alike. Far be it from you! Will not the Judge of all the earth do right?" The Lord said, "If I find fifty righteous people in the city of Sodom, I will spare the whole place for their sake."

Finally, God said He would spare the city if ten righteous people could be found in it. But ten righteous were not found. So the angels came to warn Lot. Lot warned his family, but his sons-in-law only laughed.

📖 **With the coming of dawn, the angels urged Lot, saying, "Hurry! Take your wife and your two daughters who are here, or you will be swept away when the city is punished." When he hesitated, the men grasped his hand and the hands of his wife and of his two daughters and led them safely out of the city, for the Lord was merciful to them. As soon as they had brought them out, one of them said, "Flee for your lives! Don't look back, and don't stop anywhere in the plain! Flee to the mountains or you will be swept away!"**

Lot and his wife and daughters fled to Zoar, and the Lord rained burning sulfur on Sodom and Gomorrah. Every living person and every living thing died.

📖 **But Lot's wife looked back, and she became a pillar of salt.**

■ Memory Verse:

II Thessalonians 3:3
But the Lord is faithful, and he will strengthen and protect you from the evil one.

■ Character Trait:

Repentance—sorrow for one's sin, and turning away from that sin to serve God and do right. Repentance involves admitting to God that you did something wrong, feeling sorry for that wrongdoing, and changing your behavior from wrong actions to right ones.

Abraham's Greatest Test

God fulfilled His promise to Abraham and Sarah and gave them a son.

📖 **Now the Lord was gracious to Sarah as he had said, and the Lord did for Sarah what he had promised. Sarah became pregnant and bore a son to Abraham in his old age, at the very time God had promised him. Abraham gave the name Isaac to the son Sarah bore him.**

Isaac grew, and God tested Abraham once again.

📖 **Abraham took the wood for the burnt offering and placed it on his son Isaac, and he himself carried the fire and the knife. As the two of them went on together, Isaac spoke up and said to his father Abraham, "Father?"**
"Yes, my son?" Abraham replied.
"The fire and wood are here," Isaac said, "but where is the lamb for the burnt offering?"
Abraham answered, "God himself will provide the lamb for the burnt offering, my son." And the two of them went on together.
When they reached the place God had told him about, Abraham built an altar there and arranged the wood on it. He bound his son Isaac and laid him on the altar, on top of the wood.

As Abraham took the knife to kill Isaac, the angel of the Lord called to Abraham.

📖 **"Do not lay a hand on the boy," he said. "Do not do anything to him. Now I know that you fear God, because you have not withheld from me your son, your only son."**
Abraham looked up and there in a thicket he saw a ram caught by its horns. He went over and took the ram and sacrificed it as a burnt offering instead of his son.

God renewed His covenant with Abraham, and Abraham returned to his servants.

■ **Memory Verse:**
Hebrews 11:6
And without faith it is impossible to please God, because anyone who comes to him must believe that he exists and that he rewards those who earnestly seek him.

■ **Character Trait:**
Faith—the act of believing the things that God has revealed about Himself and acting on those beliefs. People who are Christians are to live by faith.

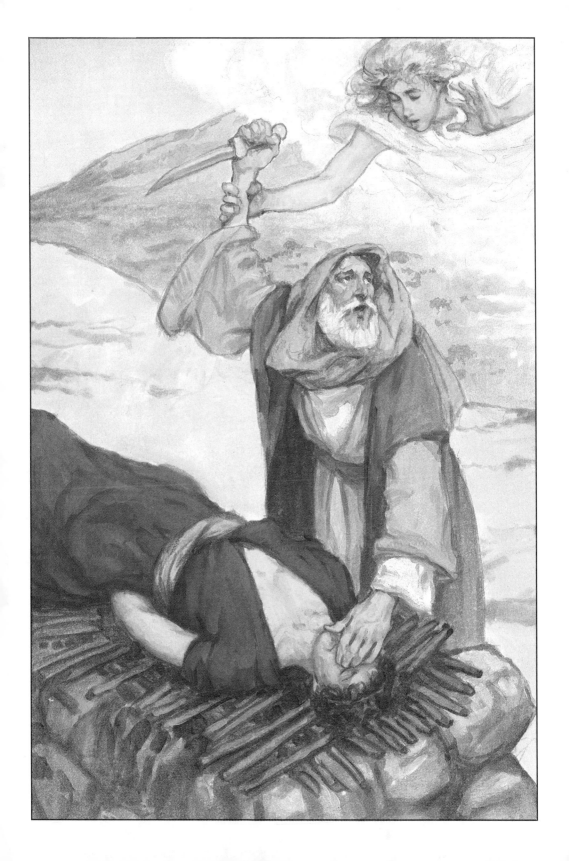

A Cause for Thankfulness

Abraham sent his servant to Haran to find a godly wife for Isaac.

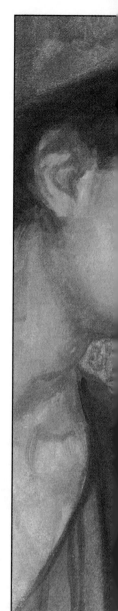

📖 Then the servant took ten of his master's camels and left, taking with him all kinds of good things from his master. He set out for Aram Naharaim and made his way to the town of Nahor. He had the camels kneel down near the well outside the town; it was toward evening, the time the women go out to draw water.

Then he prayed, "O Lord, God of my master Abraham, give me success today, and show kindness to my master Abraham. See, I am standing beside this spring, and the daughters of the townspeople are coming out to draw water. May it be that when I say to a girl, 'Please let down your jar that I may have a drink,' and she says, 'Drink, and I'll water your camels too,—let her be the one you have chosen for your servant Isaac. By this I will know that you have shown kindness to my master."

Before he had finished praying, Rebekah came out with her jar on her shoulder. She was the daughter of Bethuel son of Milcah, who was the wife of Abraham's brother Nahor. The girl was very beautiful, a virgin; no man had ever lain with her. She went down to the spring, filled her jar and came up again.

The servant hurried to meet her and said, "Please give me a little water from your jar."

"Drink, my lord," she said, and quickly lowered the jar to her hands and gave him a drink. After she had given him a drink, she said, "I'll draw water for your camels too, until they have finished drinking." So she quickly emptied her jar into the trough, ran back to the well to draw more water, and drew enough for all his camels.

Then Rebekah took Abraham's servant home to meet her family. He asked permission for Rebekah to come with him to marry Isaac. Rebekah's family let her decide. Rebekah said she would go.

📖 So they sent their sister Rebekah on her way, along with her nurse and Abraham's servant and his men.

■ Memory Verse:

Galatians 6:10
Therefore, as we have opportunity, let us do good to all people, especially to those who belong to the family of believers.

■ Character Trait:

Thankfulness—the recognition of God as the one who creates all that is good and the expression of appreciation to Him. It should be natural for us to give thanks to God.

What Makes a Winner?

After Abraham's death, the tribe continued to grow under Isaac's peaceful leadership. But gradually jealousy grew between his sons.

📖 Once when Jacob was cooking some stew, Esau came in from the open country, famished. He said to Jacob, "Quick, let me have some of that red stew! I'm famished!" (That is why he was also called Edom. Jacob replied, "First sell me your birthright."

"Look, I am about to die," Esau said. "What good is the birthright to me?"
But Jacob said, "Swear to me first." So he swore an oath to him, selling his birthright to Jacob.

Years passed. Isaac grew old and blind. When he knew he would die soon, he called Esau to him. He told Esau to kill some game and make his favorite meal. Then Isaac promised to bless Esau.

📖 So he went and got them and brought them to his mother, and she prepared some tasty food, just the way his father liked it. Then Rebekah took the best clothes of Esau her older son, which she had in the house, and put them on her younger son Jacob. She also covered his hands and the smooth part of his neck with the goatskins. Then she handed to her son Jacob the tasty food and the bread she had made.

He went to his father and said, "My father."

"Yes, my son," he answered. "Who is it?"

Jacob said to his father, "I am Esau your firstborn. I have done as you told me. Please sit up and eat some of my game so that you may give me your blessing."

Isaac touched the fleece on Jacob's arms, believed Jacob's lie and blessed him. Esau returned and discovered what Jacob had done. He was very angry. Jacob fled to Haran.

■ Memory Verse:

Philippians 2:4
Each of you should look not only to your own interests, but also to the interests of others.

■ Character Trait:

Honesty—telling the truth and not being deceitful. It is possible to tell the truth with your words, yet by your actions deceive others. If you are honest, neither your words nor your actions will mislead anyone.

The Homecoming

After twenty years, Jacob began the journey home. Jacob wondered if his brother Esau would forgive him for the mean, selfish trick he had played. He sent messengers to Esau, who was coming with 400 men. Jacob was afraid.

He [Jacob] instructed the one in the lead: "When my brother Esau meets you and asks, 'To whom do you belong, and where are you going, and who owns all these ani-mals in front of you?' then you are to say, 'They belong to your servant Jacob. They are a gift sent to my lord Esau, and he is coming behind us.' "

He also instructed the second, the third and all the others who followed the herds: "You are to say the same thing to Esau when you meet him. And be sure to say, 'Your servant Jacob is coming behind us.' " For he thought, "I will pacify him with these gifts I am sending on

■ **Memory Verse:**

Psalm 34:15
The eyes of the Lord are on the righteous and his ears are attentive to their cry.

■ **Character Trait:**

Forgiveness—forgetting or "blotting out" someone's sin and guilt. Any request for forgiveness should go with a desire to make up for the wrong.

ahead; later, when I see him, perhaps he will receive me." So Jacob's gifts went on ahead of him, but he himself spent the night in the camp.

Jacob looked up and there was Esau, coming with his four hundred men; so he divided the children among Leah, Rachel and the two maidservants. He put the maidservants and their children in front, Leah and her children next, and Rachel and Joseph in the rear. He himself went on ahead and bowed down to the ground seven times as he approached his brother. But Esau ran to meet Jacob and embraced him; he threw his arms around his neck and kissed him. And they wept.

So Esau forgave Jacob, and there was peace between them.

Brothers Divided

Jacob (renamed Israel) had a son, Joseph, whom he loved dearly. He made him a beautiful robe of many colors.

▢ When his brothers saw that their father loved him [Joseph] more than any of them, they hated him and could not speak a kind word to him.
Joseph had a dream, and when he told it to his brothers, they hated him all the more. He said to them, "Listen to this dream I had: We were binding sheaves of grain out in the field when suddenly my sheaf rose and stood upright, while your sheaves gathered around mine and bowed down to it."
His brothers said to him, "Do you intend to reign over us? Will you actually rule us?" And they hated

him all the more because of his dream and what he had said.

Then he had another dream, and he told it to his brothers. "Listen," he said, "I had another dream, and this time the sun and moon and eleven stars were bowing down to me."

When he told his father as well as his brothers, his father rebuked him and said, "What is this dream you had? Will your mother and I and your brothers actually come and bow down to the ground before you?" His brothers were jealous of him, but his father kept the matter in mind.

Joseph's brothers were jealous. They took his robe and threw Joseph into a well. A caravan of Ishmaelites from Gilead came. So the brothers sold Joseph to the Ishmaelites. The brothers told Jacob that Joseph was dead, showing him Joseph's coat that they had dipped in blood. Jacob mourned.

■ Memory Verse:

Romans 12:15
Rejoice with those who rejoice; mourn with those who mourn.

■ Character Trait:

Loyalty—a strong devotion to a person or ideal. True loyalty is a willingness to stand by your friends and your beliefs when no one else seems ready to do so.

Tough Faith

Joseph was taken to Egypt. He became a servant in the home of Potiphar, the captain of Pharoah's guard. Potiphar trusted Joseph and treated him well. Joseph, a handsome young man, was in charge of all Potiphar's house.

📖 **And after a while his master's wife took notice of Joseph and said, "Come to bed with me!"**
But he refused. "With me in charge," he told her, "my master does not concern himself with anything in the house; everything he owns he has entrusted to my care. No one is greater in this house than I am. My master has withheld nothing from me except you, because you are his wife. How then could I do such a wicked thing and sin against God?" And though she spoke to Joseph day after day, he refused to go to bed with her or even be with her.
One day he went into the house to attend to his duties, and none of the household servants was inside. She caught him by his cloak and said, "Come to bed with me!" But he left his cloak in her hand and ran out of the house.

Potiphar's wife lied to the servants and to her husband. Potiphar was very angry and had Joseph thrown in prison. One night, two prisoners—a royal cupbearer and a baker who had displeased Pharaoh—dreamed puzzling dreams. Joseph told them what their dreams meant.

The cupbearer would be pardoned to serve Pharaoh again, and the baker would be hanged. Joseph's predictions came true. But the cupbearer forgot about Joseph.

📖 **When two full years had passed, Pharaoh had a dream: He was standing by the Nile, when out of the river there came up seven cows, sleek and fat, and they grazed among the reeds. After them, seven other cows, ugly and gaunt, came up out of the Nile and stood beside those on the riverbank. And the cows that were ugly and gaunt ate up the seven sleek, fat cows. Then Pharaoh woke up.**
He fell asleep again and had a second dream: Seven heads of grain, healthy and good, were growing on a single stalk. After them, seven other heads of grain sprouted—thin and scorched by the east wind. The thin heads of grain swallowed up the seven healthy, full heads. Then Pharaoh woke up; it had been a dream.

Pharaoh was troubled. No one could tell him what the dreams meant. But his cupbearer remembered Joseph. Joseph told Pharaoh to prepare for seven years of abundance followed by seven years of famine. God blessed Joseph.

📖 **Then Pharaoh said to Joseph, "Since God has made all this known to you, there is no one so discerning and wise as you. You shall be in charge of my palace, and all my people are to submit to your orders. Only with respect to the throne will I be greater than you." So Pharaoh said to Joseph, "I hereby put you in charge of the whole land of Egypt."**

■ **Memory Verse:**

I Corinthians 15:58
Therefore, my dear brothers, stand firm. Let nothing move you. Always give yourselves fully to the work of the Lord, because you know that your labor in the Lord is not in vain.

■ **Character Trait:**

Faith—believing what God has said about Himself and acting on those beliefs. Joseph knew God would not forget him. Faith is the certainty that what we hope for is waiting for us.

Family Reunion

When a great famine came, Joseph's brothers traveled to Egypt to buy food. The brothers didn't recognize Joseph, but Joseph knew his brothers at once. Joseph, however, pretended to be a stranger. He accused them of being spies.

📖 But they replied, "Your servants were twelve brothers, the sons of one man, who lives in the land of Canaan. The youngest is now with our father, and one is no more." Joseph said to them, "It is just as I told you: You are spies! And this is how you will be tested: As surely as Pharaoh lives, you will not leave this place unless your youngest brother comes here. Send one of your number to get your brother; the rest of you will be kept in prison, so that your words may be tested to

see if you are telling the truth. If you are not, then as surely as Pharaoh lives, you are spies!" And he put them all in custody for three days.

📖 When Joseph saw Benjamin with them, he said to the steward of his house, "Take these men to my house, slaughter an animal and prepare dinner; they are to eat with me at noon."

So they [the brothers] went up to Joseph's steward and spoke to him at the entrance to the house. "Please, sir," they said, "we came down here the first time to buy food. But at the place where we stopped for the night we opened our sacks and each of us found his silver—the exact weight—in the mouth of his sack. So we have brought it back with us. We have also brought additional silver with us to buy food. We don't know who put our silver in our sacks."

"It's all right," he said. "Don't be afraid. Your God, the God of your father, has given you treasure in your sacks; I received your silver." Then he brought Simeon out to them.

The brothers were horrified and begged for their service in exchange for Benjamin's release.

📖 Then Joseph could no longer control himself before all his attendants, and he cried out, "Have everyone leave my presence!" So there was no one with Joseph when he made himself known to his brothers. And he wept so loudly that the Egyptians heard him, and Pharaoh's household heard about it.

Joseph said to his brothers, "I am Joseph! Is my father still living?" But his brothers were not able to answer him, because they were terrified at his presence.

Then Joseph said to his brothers, "Come close to me." When they had done so, he said, "I am your brother Joseph, the one you sold into Egypt! And now, do not be distressed and do not be angry with yourselves for selling me here, because it was to save lives that God sent me ahead of you."

Joseph forgave his brothers and sent them back to Canaan to bring Jacob and all their families to Egypt.

■ **Memory Verse:**
Matthew 5:44
But I tell you: Love your enemies and pray for those who persecute you.

■ **Character Trait:**
Forgiveness—forgetting or blotting out someone's sin and guilt. Any request for forgiveness should go with a desire to make up for the wrong. Sometimes it is difficult for us to forgive others, but to forgive is always the right thing to do.

A Sea Divided

God had chosen Moses to deliver his people, Israel, from Pharaoh in Egypt. When all the firstborn Egyptian children died one night, Pharaoh agreed to let Israel go. God led Israel around by the desert road toward the Red Sea.

By day the LORD went ahead of them in a pillar of cloud to guide them on their way and by night in a pillar of fire to give them light, so that they could travel by day or night. Neither the pillar of cloud by day nor the pillar of fire by night left its place in front of the people.

When Pharaoh was told Israel had fled, God hardened Pharaoh's heart against them. Pharaoh and his officers changed their minds and chased Israel.

The LORD hardened the heart of Pharaoh king of Egypt, so that he pursued the Israelites, who were marching out boldly. The Egyptians—all Pharaoh's horses and chariots, horsemen and troops—pursued the Israelites and overtook them as they camped by the sea near Pi Hahiroth, opposite Baal Zephon.

Israel was terrified and accused Moses of bringing them to the desert to die. Moses told them not to be afraid because the Lord would deliver them.

The LORD will fight for you; you need only to be still." Then the LORD said to Moses, "Why are you crying out to me? Tell the Israelites to move on. Raise your staff and stretch out your hand over the sea to divide the water so that the Israelites can go through the sea on dry ground."

God again hardened the hearts of the Egyptians so they would go into the sea after Israel.

I will harden the hearts of the Egyptians so that they will go in after them. And I will gain glory through Pharaoh and all his army, through his chariots and his horsemen. The Egyptians will know that I am the LORD when I gain glory through Pharaoh, his chariots and his horsemen."
Then the angel of God, who had been traveling in front of Israel's army, withdrew and went behind them. The pillar of cloud also moved from in front and stood behind them, coming between the armies of Egypt and Israel. Throughout the night the cloud brought darkness to the one side and light to the other side; so neither went near the other all night long.

Then Moses stretched out his hand over the sea, and all that night the LORD drove the sea back with a strong east wind and turned it into dry land. The waters were divided, and the Israelites went through the sea on dry ground, with a wall of water on their right and on their left.

The Egyptians pursued them. The Lord confused the army and made the wheels of the chariots come off!

📖 Then the LORD said to Moses, "Stretch out your hand over the sea so that the waters may flow back over the Egyptians and their chariots and horsemen." Moses stretched out his hand over the sea, and at daybreak the sea went back to its place. The Egyptians were fleeing toward it, and the LORD swept them into the sea.

The water covered the chariots and horsemen. None of them survived.

■ Memory Verse:

Hebrews 11:1
Now faith is being sure of what we hope for and certain of what we do not see.

■ Character Trait:

Confidence—a feeling of security based on faith and trust. It is the belief that God will take care of you in any situation—no matter what the circumstances. Moses had confidence in God's ability to deliver Israel from the Egyptians.

Tablets of Stone

After the nation of Israel left Egypt, God spoke to them through Moses. He took Moses up to a mountain and wrote laws on two stone tablets for the people to obey . These laws were called the Ten Commandments. Moses came down from the mountain and read the laws to the people.

📖 "You shall have no other gods before me.

"You shall not make for yourself an idol in the form of anything in heaven above or on the earth beneath or in the waters below. You shall not bow down to them or worship them; for I, the LORD your God, am a jealous God, punishing the children for the sin of the fathers to the third and fourth generation of those who hate me, but showing love to a thousand [generations] of those who love me and keep my commandments.

"You shall not misuse the name of the LORD your God, for the LORD will not hold anyone guiltless who misuses his name.

"Observe the Sabbath day by keeping it holy, as the LORD your God has commanded you.

"Honor your father and your mother, as the LORD your God has commanded you, so that you may live long and that it may go well with you in the land the LORD your God is giving you.

"You shall not murder.

"You shall not commit adultery.

"You shall not steal.

"You shall not give false testimony against your neighbor.

"You shall not covet your neighbor's wife. You shall not set your desire on your neighbor's house or land, his manservant or maidservant, his ox or donkey, or anything that belongs to your neighbor."

■ Memory Verse:

II Peter 1:21
For prophecy never had its origin in the will of man, but men spoke from God as they were carried along by the Holy Spirit.

■ Character Trait:

Obedience—doing what you are told to do. We are commanded to be obedient to God in every way. Obedience is part of our faith because it shows we know that God can teach us and protect us.

Jericho's Falling Out

Rahab, a harlot in Jericho, hid two Hebrew spies and helped them escape, disobeying the King of Jericho's orders. In return, the spies promised to spare her life and those within her house when Israel attacked. After the spies returned with a report on the city, God told the Israelites how to attack successfully.

📖 **Now Jericho was tightly shut up because of the Israelites. No one went out and no one came in. Then the LORD said to Joshua, "See, I have delivered Jericho into your hands, along with its king and its fighting men. March around the city once with all the armed men. Do this for six days. Have seven priests**

carry trumpets of rams' horns in front of the ark. On the seventh day, march around the city seven times, with the priests blowing the trumpets. When you hear them sound a long blast on the trumpets, have all the people give a loud shout; then the wall of the city will collapse and the people will go up, every man straight in."

Joshua and Israel did as God commanded. The walls of Jericho collapsed. As further proof of God's miracle, the walls fell outward, rather than inward. Victory belonged to Israel. Rahab's life was spared as the spies had promised.

■ Memory Verse:

2 Corinthians 5:7
We live by faith, not by sight.

■ Character Trait:

Courage—the ability and willingness to stand firm when confronted by danger, fear, or peer pressure. Some of the Bible's best examples of courage come from situations where someone knows the right thing to do and does it, even when afraid or in danger. Rahab displayed courage when she hid the spies. Joshua and Israel had the courage to obey God and believe Him for the victory.

Unlikely Hero

Gideon was a farmer, but God was calling him to do something great.

📖 Gideon said to God, "If you will save Israel by my hand as you have promised—look, I will place a wool fleece on the threshing floor. If there is dew only on the fleece and all the ground is dry, then I will know that you will save Israel by my hand, as you said." And that is what hap-

pened. Gideon rose early the next day; he squeezed the fleece and wrung out the dew—a bowlful of water. Then Gideon said to God, "Do not be angry with me. Let me make just one more request. Allow me one more test with the fleece. This time make the fleece dry and the ground covered with dew." That night God did so. Only the fleece was dry; all the ground was covered with dew.

■ **Memory Verse:**

Isaiah 14:24
The Lord Almighty has sworn, "Surely, as I have planned, so it will be, and as I have purposed, so it will stand."

■ **Character Trait:**

Courage—the ability and willingness to stand firm when confronted by danger, fear, or peer pressure. Sometimes it may be more courageous to endure temporary defeat or failure than to use force to do away with it.

Blaze of Glory

Israel was getting ready for a battle with the Midianites

📖 Early in the morning, Jerub-Baal (that is, Gideon) and all his men camped at the spring of Harod. The camp of Midian was north of them in the valley near the hill of Moreh. The LORD said to Gideon, "You have too many men for me to deliver Midian into their hands. In order that Israel may not boast against me that her own strength has saved her, announce now to the people, 'Anyone who trembles with fear may turn back and leave Mount Gilead.'" So twenty-two thousand men left, while ten thousand remained.

God said there were still too many men.

📖 So Gideon took the men down to the water. There the LORD told him, "Separate those who lap the water with their tongues like a dog from those who kneel down to drink." Three hundred men lapped with their hands to their mouths. All the

rest got down on their knees to drink. The LORD said to Gideon, "With the three hundred men that lapped I will save you and give the Midianites into your hands. Let all the other men go, each to his own place." So Gideon sent the rest of the Israelites to their tents but kept the three hundred, who took over the provisions and trumpets of the others.

During the night, the Lord told Gideon to attack the Midianites. Gideon and his servant Purah spied on the Midianites. The Midianites were afraid of Gideon. So Gideon and his 300 men attacked. They blew their trumpets and broke their jars.

📖 **The three companies blew the trumpets and smashed the jars. Grasping the torches in their left hands and holding in their right hands the trumpets they were to blow, they shouted, "A sword for the LORD and for Gideon!" While each man held his position around the camp, all the Midianites ran, crying out as they fled.**

The Lord caused the Midianites to kill each other with their swords.

■ **Memory Verse:**

I Corinthians 1:27
But God chose the foolish things of the world to shame the wise; God chose the weak things of the world to shame the strong.

■ **Character Trait:**

Courage—the ability to stand firm when confronted by danger, fear, or peer pressure. Some of the Bible's best examples of courage come from situations where someone knew the right thing to do and did it, even when afraid or in danger.

A Giant Bites the Dust

For forty days the Philistine giant, Goliath, challenged Israel to fight. But not one soldier in all of King Saul's army was brave enough to accept the challenge, until David, a young shepherd, offered to meet the giant with a staff, a sling, and his faith in God.

As the Philistine moved closer to attack him, David ran quickly toward the battle line to meet him. Reaching into his bag and taking out a stone, he slung it and struck the Philistine on the forehead. The stone sank into his forehead, and

■ **Memory Verse:**

Psalm 27:1
The Lord is my light and my salvation—whom shall I fear? The Lord is the stronghold of my life—of whom shall I be afraid?

■ **Character Trait:**

Courage—the ability and willingness to stand firm when confronted by danger, fear, or peer pressure. The basis of courage is not usually physical strength, but rather a mental or moral strength.

he fell facedown on the ground. So David triumphed over the Philistine with a sling and a stone; without a sword in his hand he struck down the Philistine and killed him. David ran and stood over him. He took hold of the Philistine's sword and drew it from the scabbard. After he killed him, he cut off his head with the sword. When the Philistines saw that their hero was dead, they turned and ran.

Attempted Murder

After David killed Goliath, Saul kept David with him. Jonathan and David became best friends. David was given a high rank in the army. God gave David success.

📖 When the men were returning home after David had killed the Philistine, the women came out from all the towns of Israel to meet King Saul with singing and dancing, with joyful songs and with tambourines and lutes. As they danced, they sang: "Saul has slain his thousands, and David his tens of thousands." Saul was very angry; this refrain galled him. "They have credited David with tens of thousands," he thought, "but me with only thousands. What more can he get but the kingdom?" And from that time on Saul kept a jealous eye on David.

King Saul was so jealous that he threw a spear at David while David played his harp for the king. But David escaped twice.

📖 Saul was afraid of David, because the LORD was with David but had left Saul. So he sent David away from him and gave him command over a thousand men, and David led the troops in their campaigns.
In everything he did he had great success, because the LORD was with him. When Saul saw how successful he was, he was afraid of him. But all Israel and Judah loved David, because he led them in their campaigns.

■ Memory Verse:
Psalm 138:8a
The Lord will fulfill [his purpose] for me; your love, O Lord, endures forever.

■ Character Trait:
Confidence—a feeling of security based on faith and trust. It is the firm belief that God can see you safely through any situation—no matter what.

53

Friendship Factor

Saul was in Ramah. While he was there, David hurried back to the palace to see Jonathan. Jonathan agreed to find out if Saul still wanted to kill David and why. He planned to send word to David.

📖 **So Jonathan made a covenant with the house of David, saying, "May the Lord call David's enemies to account."**

Saul knew Jonathan loved David. He was angry, and threw a spear at Jonathan.

📖 **In the morning Jonathan went out to the field for his meeting with David. He had a small boy with him, and he said to the boy, "Run and find the arrows I shoot." As the boy ran, he shot an arrow beyond him. When the boy came to the place where Jonathan's arrow had fallen, Jonathan called out after him, "Isn't the arrow beyond you?" Then he shouted, "Hurry! Go quickly! Don't stop!" The boy picked up the arrow and returned to his master. (The boy knew nothing of all this; only Jonathan and David knew.) Then Jonathan** gave his weapons to the boy and said, "Go, carry them back to town." After the boy had gone, David got up from the south side [of the stone] and bowed down before Jonathan three times, with his face to the ground. Then they kissed each other and wept together—but David wept the most.

Jonathan said to David, "Go in peace, for we have sworn friendship with each other in the name of the LORD, saying, 'The LORD is witness between you and me, and between your descendants and my descendants forever.'" Then David left, and Jonathan went back to the town.

■ Memory Verse:

Ephesians 2:10
For we are God's workmanship, created in Christ Jesus to do good works, which God prepared in advance for us to do.

■ Character Trait:

Friendliness—a mutual feeling of affection between two people. In addition to our human friendships, it is possible to be a friend of God.

On the Run

David fled for his life. Saul went after him with three thousand men. Saul stopped in a cave unaware that David and his men are hiding in it. David carefully cut off a piece of Saul's robe. Saul later left the cave and David called to him, holding up the piece of robe. Saul pretended to be sorry.

When David finished saying this, Saul asked, "Is that your voice, David my son?" And he wept aloud. "You are more righteous than I," he said. "You have treated me well, but I have treated you badly. You have just now told me of the good you did to me; the Lord delivered me into your hands, but you did not kill me. When a man finds his enemy, does he let him get away unharmed? May the Lord reward you well for the way you treated me today. I know

that you will surely be king and that the kingdom of Israel will be established in your hands. Now swear to me by the Lord that you will not cut off my descendants or wipe out my name from my father's family."
So David gave his oath to Saul. Then Saul returned home, but David and his men went up to the stronghold.

■ Memory Verse:

Romans 12:21
Do not be overcome by evil, but overcome evil with good.

■ Character Trait:

Peacefulness—the sense of feeling at rest even though you may be experiencing difficult circumstances. When the Bible refers to peace, the definition is more than being free from war or disorder. Peacefulness is the assurance that God hasn't deserted you and that everything is still okay.

Wrong Way Up

Messengers told King David that his son Absalom had killed all of his brothers. But David sons rushed to their father, bringing him news that Absalom had killed only Amnon. After three years, David who missed Absalom, sent General Joab to bring Absalom to David in Jerusalem.

Absalom lived two years in Jerusalem without seeing the king's face...

Absalom said to Joab, "Look, I sent word to you and said, 'Come here so I can send you to the king to ask, "Why have I come from Geshur? It would be better for me if I were still there!" ' Now then, I want to see the king's face, and if I am guilty of anything, let him put me to death." So Joab went to the king and told him this. Then the king summoned Absalom, and he came in and bowed down with his face to

the ground before the king. And the king kissed Absalom.

But Absalom planned to steal David's throne. Fearful that Jerusalem would support Absalom, David gathered his army and fled. He left his wisest military man, Hushai, in the palace to spy on Absalom.

📖 Absalom asked Hushai, "Is this the love you show your friend? Why didn't you go with your friend?" Hushai said to Absalom, "No, the one chosen by the LORD, by these people, and by all the men of Israel—his I will be, and I will remain with him. Furthermore, whom should I serve? Should I not serve the son? Just as I served your father, so I will serve you."

Absalom believed Husha. He advised Absalom not to attack David yet. Meanwhile, David organized his army. Messengers have been sent to warn David of Absalom's plan. Later, David and Absalom's armies met. Absalom's army was defeated.

📖 When one of the men saw this, he told Joab, "I just saw Absalom hanging in an oak tree." Joab said to the man who had told him this, "What! You saw him? Why didn't you strike him to the ground right there? Then I would have had to give you ten shekels of silver and a warrior's belt."

But the man replied, "Even if a thousand shekels were weighed out into my hands, I would not lift my hand against the king's son. In our hearing the king commanded you and Abishai and Ittai, 'Protect the young man Absalom for my sake.' And if I had put my life in jeopardy—and nothing is hidden from the king—you would have kept your distance from me."

Joab said, "I'm not going to wait like this for you." So he took three javelins in his hand and plunged them into Absalom's heart while Absalom was still alive in the oak tree. And ten of Joab's armor-bearers surrounded Absalom, struck him and killed him.

Then Joab sounded the trumpet, and the troops stopped pursuing Israel, for Joab halted them. They took Absalom, threw him into a big pit in the forest and piled up a large heap of rocks over him. Meanwhile, all the Israelites fled to their homes.

■ Memory Verse:
Leviticus 19:11
" 'Do not steal. Do not lie. Do not deceive one another.' "

■ Character Trait:
Loyalty—a strong devotion to a person or ideal. True loyalty is a willingness to stand by your friends and your beliefs when no one else is willing to do so.

The Choice

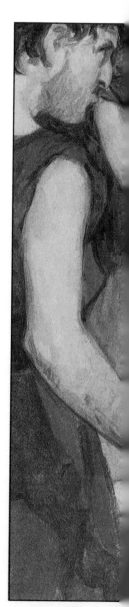

King Solomon, David's son, was the wisest man that ever lived. His wisdom was tested greatly when two women were arguing over a baby. One woman's baby had died. The other woman's baby lived. Each woman claimed to be the mother of the living child.

📖 The king said, "This one says, 'My son is alive and your son is dead,' while that one says, 'No! Your son is dead and mine is alive.'" Then the king said, "Bring me a sword." So they brought a sword for the king. He then gave an order: "Cut the living child in two and give half to one and half to the other." The woman whose son was alive was filled with compassion for her son and said to the king, "Please, my lord, give her the living baby! Don't kill him!"

But the other said, "Neither I nor you shall have him. Cut him in two!"

Then the king gave his ruling: "Give the living baby to the first woman. Do not kill him; she is his mother."

When all Israel heard the verdict the king had given, they held the king in awe, because they saw that he had wisdom from God to administer justice.

■ **Memory Verse:**

Proverbs 3:5
Trust in the Lord with all your heart and lean not on your own understanding.

■ **Character Trait:**

Resourcefulness—the ability to devise ways and means of getting a job accomplished. A resourceful person takes every opportunity to make the most of his or her abilities, resources, and situations.

A Queen Comes to Call

God had blessed Solomon with wisdom and wealth second to none. The Queen of Sheba heard about Solomon and decided to visit Jerusalem to see if what she had heard was true.

📖 When the queen of Sheba saw all the wisdom of Solomon and the palace he had built, the food on his table, the seating of his officials, the attending servants in their robes, his cupbearers, and the burnt offerings he made at the temple of the Lord, she was overwhelmed.
She said to the king, "The report I heard in my own country about your achievements and your wisdom is true. But I did not believe these things until I came and saw with my own eyes. Indeed, not even half was told me; in wisdom and wealth you have far exceeded the report I heard. How happy your men must be! How happy your officials, who continually stand before you and hear your wisdom! Praise be to the Lord your God, who has delighted in you and placed you on the throne of Israel.

Because of the Lord's eternal love for Israel, he has made you king, to maintain justice and righteousness."

God was pleased with Solomon's faithful service. He caused the King's fame and influence to increase.

■ Memory Verse:
1 Samuel 12:24
But be sure to fear the Lord and serve him faithfully with all your heart; consider what great things he has done for you.

■ Character Trait:
Wisdom—includes more than just knowing facts. It also includes skills, common sense, good judgment, and godly living. God is the source of wisdom, and a healthy respect for Him is the starting point for those who wish to be wise.

The Contest

Israel was in the middle of a great famine. The prophet Elijah went to meet wicked King Ahab, who blamed Elijah for the famine.

📖 "I have not made trouble for Israel," Elijah replied. "But you and your father's family have. You have abandoned the Lord's commands and have followed the Baals. Now summon the people from all over Israel to meet me on Mount Carmel. And bring the four hundred and fifty prophets of Baal and the four hundred prophets of Asherah, who eat at Jezebel's table."

So the prophets of Baal gathered on Mt. Carmel. They prepared a sacrifice, chanted, and called upon their god for many hours. Baal, their god, did not answer. At last they gave up. Then Elijah prepared an altar and dug a trench around it. He prepared his sacrifice.

📖 He arranged the wood, cut the bull into pieces and laid it on the wood. Then he said to them, "Fill four large jars with water and pour it on the offering and on the wood." "Do it again," he said, and they did it again.
"Do it a third time," he ordered, and they did it the third time. The water ran down around the altar and even filled the trench.
At the time of sacrifice, the prophet Elijah stepped forward and prayed: "O Lord, God of Abraham, Isaac and Israel, let it be known today that you are God in Israel and that I am your servant and have done all these things at your command. Answer me, O Lord, answer me, so these people will know that you, O Lord, are God, and that you are turning their hearts back again."
Then the fire of the Lord fell and burned up the sacrifice, the wood, the stones and the soil, and also licked up the water in the trench.

Then all the people knew Elijah's God was the true God. All the prophets of Baal were

killed. A small cloud the size of a man's hand appeared in the sky. Soon a great storm came, and the famine was ended.

■ Memory Verse:

Jeremiah 10:10a
But the Lord is the true God; he is the living God, the eternal King.

■ Character Trait:

Confidence—a feeling of security based on faith and trust. It is the firm belief that God can see you safely through any situation, no matter what. Real confidence is based on God's ability to take care of you.

Down and Out in Desert Caves

Queen Jezebel became very angry with Elijah because he had defeated the prophets of Baal and had had them killed. Afraid, Elijah ran for his life. God asked Elijah why he was hiding.

He replied, "I have been very zealous for the Lord God Almighty. The Israelites have rejected your covenant, broken down your altars, and put your prophets to death with the sword. I am the only one left, and now they are trying to kill me too."

The Lord said to him, "Go back the way you came, and go to the Desert of Damascus. When you get there, anoint Hazael king over

Aram. Also, anoint Jehu son of Nimshi king over Israel, and anoint Elisha son of Shaphat from Abel Meholah to succeed you as prophet. Jehu will put to death any who escape the sword of Hazael, and Elisha will put to death any who escape the sword of Jehu. Yet I reserve seven thousand in Israel—all whose knees have not bowed down to Baal and all whose mouths have not kissed him."

■ Memory Verse:

Proverbs 19:21
Many are the plans in a man's heart, but it is the Lord's purpose that prevails.

■ Character Trait:

Perseverance—the ability to keep on going even under pressure without becoming discouraged. Perseverance does not take place without some kind of obstacle or persecution. Since none of us can avoid trouble entirely, it is important to develop perseverance.

You Asked for It

Elisha asked for a double portion of Elijah's power.

📖 "You have asked a difficult thing," Elijah said, "yet if you see me when I am taken from you, it will be yours—otherwise not."

As they were walking along and talking together, suddenly a chariot of fire and horses of fire appeared and separated the two of them, and Elijah went up to heaven in a whirlwind. Elisha saw this and cried out, "My father! My father! The chariots and horsemen of Israel!" And Elisha saw him no more. Then he took hold of his own clothes and tore them apart. He picked up the cloak that had fallen from Elijah and went back and stood on the bank of the Jordan.

◼ Memory Verse:

Psalm 40:8
I desire to do your will, O my God; your law is within my heart.

◼ Character Trait:

Trust—an unwavering belief in someone or something, especially when dealing with standards such as truth, strength, or character. To put your trust in God means to rely on Him to get you through any situation, no matter how difficult it is.

■ 2 Kings 6:16—19, 23a

Chariots of Fire

The king of Syria sent a great army to Dothan to capture Elisha. When Elisha's servant woke up the next morning, he saw troops, horses, and chariots everywhere. He cried to Elisha with fear.

📖 "Don't be afraid," the prophet answered. "Those who are with us are more than those who are with them."
And Elisha prayed, "O LORD, open his eyes so he may see." Then the LORD **opened the servant's eyes, and he looked and saw the hills full** of horses and chariots of fire all around Elisha.
As the enemy came down toward him, Elisha prayed to the LORD, "Strike these people with blindness." So he struck them with blindness, as Elisha had asked.
Elisha told them, "This is not the road and this is not the city. Follow me, and I will lead you to the man you are looking for." And he led them to Samaria.

As soon as the Syrian army arrived, God opened their eyes. They discov-

ered they were in Samaria, the capital of Israel. But Elisha asked the King of Israel to spare the lives of the Syrian army.

📖 **So he prepared a great feast for them, and after they had finished eating and drinking, he sent them away, and they returned to their master.**

The Syrian army didn't bother Israel again.

■ Memory Verse:

Psalm 34:7
The angel of the Lord encamps around those who fear him, and he delivers them.

■ Character Trait:

Confidence—a feeling of security based on faith and trust. It is the firm belief that God can see you safely through any situation. Elisha knew he was surrounded by God's protecting power.

Solomon's Temple Dedication

Solomon's temple was finally finished. The king held a great celebration. A parade began the event, with the king at the head, followed by priests carrying the ark of the covenant. Hundreds of sheep and cattle were sacrificed to the Lord as priests carried the ark to the temple. Musicians played and everyone sang praises to God.

📖 **Then the temple of the LORD was filled with a cloud, and the priests could not perform their service because of the cloud, for the glory of the LORD filled the temple of God.**

When Solomon saw what had happened, he praised God and dedicated the temple to Him.

📖 **Then Solomon stood before the altar of the LORD in front of the whole assembly of Israel and spread out his hands.**

He said: "O LORD, God of Israel, there is no God like you in heaven or on earth—you who keep your covenant of love with your servants who continue wholeheart-edly in your way. You have kept your promise to your servant David my father; with your mouth you have promised and with your hand you have fulfilled it—as it is today.**

Solomon's temple remained an important part of Israel's history. According to Biblical prophecy, the temple will be rebuilt someday.

■ **Memory Verse:**
John 14:15
"If you love me, you will obey what I command."

■ **Character Trait:**
Worship—to honor and adore someone who is worthy of high honor. True worship involves not only things we do, but also our thoughts and feelings as we do them. Only God fully deserves our worship.

A Queen to the Rescue

Queen Esther broke a law by appearing uninvited before the king—an act punishable by death. But the lives of her people, the Jews, were in danger, and she was the only one who could save them.

📖 Then the king asked, "What is it, Queen Esther? What is your request? Even up to half the kingdom, it will be given you."

"If it pleases the king," replied Esther, "let the king, together with Haman, come today to a banquet I have prepared for him."

"Bring Haman at once," the king said, "so that we may do what Esther asks."

So the king and Haman went to the banquet Esther had prepared. As they were drinking wine, the king again asked Esther, "Now what is your petition? It will be given you. And what is your request? Even up to half the kingdom, it will be granted."

Esther replied, "My petition and my request is this: If the king regards me with favor and if it pleases the king to grant my petition and fulfill my request, let the king and Haman come tomorrow to the banquet I will prepare for them. Then I will answer the king's question."

That night the king could not sleep.

So he ordered the book of Chronicles to be read. There he discovered that Mordecai, Esther's cousin, had saved the king's life, and nothing had been done to reward him.

📖 The king said, "Who is in the court?" Now Haman had just entered the outer court of the palace to speak to the king about hanging Mordecai on the gallows he had erected for him.

His attendants answered, "Haman is standing in the court."

"Bring him in," the king ordered.

When Haman entered, the king asked him, "What should be done for the man the king delights to honor?"

Now Haman thought to himself, "Who is there that the king would rather honor than me?" So he answered the king, "For the man the king delights to honor, have them bring a royal robe the king has worn and a horse the king has ridden, one with a royal crest placed on its head. Then let the robe and horse be entrusted to one of the king's most noble princes. Let them robe the man the king delights to honor, and lead him on the horse through the city streets, proclaiming before him, 'This is what is done for the man the king delights to honor!' "

The king ordered Haman to give

such an honor to Mordecai. Later, the king and Haman went to dine with Queen Esther. Once again the king asked Esther what her petition was. Queen Esther told the king that someone was trying to annihilate her people, the Jews.

King Xerxes asked Queen Esther, "Who is he? Where is the man who has dared to do such a thing?"
Esther said, "The adversary and enemy is this vile Haman."
Then Haman was terrified before the king and queen.

The king left in a rage, and Haman stayed behind to beg Esther for his life.

The king said, "Hang him on it!" So they hanged Haman on the gallows he had prepared for Mordecai. Then the king's fury subsided.

Later, Mordecai was given the king's signet ring, and was appointed over Haman's estate. King Xerxes made a new law giving all the Jews the right to arm and defend themselves. God's people were saved because of Queen Esther.

■ Memory Verse:

Philippians 1:27a
Whatever happens, conduct yourselves in a manner worthy of the gospel of Christ.

■ Character Trait:

Courage—the ability to stand firm when confronted by danger, fear, or peer pressure. Some of the Bible's best examples of courage came from situations in which someone knew the right thing to do and did it, even when he or she was afraid or in danger.

A Meeting with God

Judah had turned from God and had become greedy and dishonest. Enemy nations threatened her. Isaiah was a young man when he went to the temple to pray for his country, Judah.

📖 In the year that King Uzziah died, I saw the LORD seated on a throne, high and exalted, and the train of his robe filled the temple. Above him were seraphs, each with six wings: With two wings they covered their faces, with two they covered their feet, and with two they were flying. And they were calling to one another:

"Holy, holy, holy is the LORD Almighty;
the whole earth is full of his glory."
At the sound of their voices the doorposts and thresholds shook and the temple was filled with smoke.

Isaiah was terrified and bowed to worship God. He knew he was sinful and unworthy to be in God's presence.

📖 Then one of the seraphs flew to me with a live coal in his hand, which he had taken with tongs from the altar. With it he touched my mouth and said, "See, this has touched your lips; your guilt is taken away and your sin atoned for."

God chose Isaiah to be a prophet and to influence Judah to repent.

■ Memory Verse:
Romans 3:23
For all have sinned and fall short of the glory of God.

■ Character Trait:
Holiness—the condition of something or someone that is set apart as sacred or dedicated. God and Jesus are holy because they are without sin. But people can be holy as they are used for God's purposes.

76

Calm in Calamity

Job was the richest man in Uz. Satan questioned Job's faithfulness to God. God gave Satan permission to take his wealth and health, but not his life.

📖 A messenger came to Job and said, "The oxen were plowing and the donkeys were grazing nearby, and the Sabeans attacked and carried them off. They put the servants to the sword, and I am the only one who has escaped to tell you!"

While he was still speaking, another messenger came and said, "The fire of God fell from the sky and burned up the sheep and the servants, and I am the only one who has escaped to tell you!"

While he was still speaking, another messenger came and said, "The Chaldeans formed three raiding

parties and swept down on your camels and carried them off. They put the servants to the sword, and I am the only one who has escaped to tell you!"

While he was still speaking, yet another messenger came and said, "Your sons and daughters were feasting and drinking wine at the oldest brother's house, when suddenly a mighty wind swept in from the desert and struck the four corners of the house. It collapsed on them and they are dead, and I am the only one who has escaped to tell you!"

At this, Job got up and tore his robe and shaved his head. Then he fell to the ground in worship and said:

"Naked I came from my mother's womb, and naked I will depart. The LORD gave and the LORD has taken away; may the name of the LORD be praised."

In all this, Job did not sin by charging God with wrongdoing.

Job's friends told him his problems were punishment by God for sin. Job still trusted God. Finally, God spoke to Job. . . .

📖 "Who is this that darkens my counsel with words without knowledge?

Brace yourself like a man; I will question you, and you shall answer me.

"Where were you when I laid the earth's foundation?

Tell me, if you understand.

Who marked off its dimensions? Surely you know!

Who stretched a measuring line across it?

On what were its footings set, or who laid its cornerstone— while the morning stars sang together and all the angels shouted for joy?

Job worshipped God and said:

📖 I know that you can do all things; no plan of yours can be thwarted. You asked, 'Who is this that obscures my counsel without knowledge?' Surely I spoke of things I did not understand, things too wonderful for me to know. "You said, 'Listen now, and I will speak; I will question you, and you shall answer me.' My ears had heard of you but now my ears have seen you. Therefore I despise myself and repent in dust and ashes.

Job knew he had no right to question God's dealings with him, no matter what Job's circumstances. He realized God knows everything, and always knows what is best.

■ Memory Verse:

Psalm 18:30

As for God, his way is perfect; the word of the Lord is flawless. He is a shield for all who take refuge in him.

■ Character Trait:

Perseverance—the ability to keep going under pressure without becoming discouraged.

Thanks, But No Thanks

Daniel and his friends were taken as prisoners to Babylon. They were given a chance to try for positions in King Nebuchadnezzar's court. Only the smartest and strongest could pass the tests.

📖 The king assigned them a daily amount of food and wine from the king's table. They were to be trained for three years, and after that they were to enter the king's service. Among these were some from Judah: Daniel, Hananiah, Mishael and Azariah. The chief official gave them new names: to Daniel, the name Belteshazzar; to Hananiah, Shadrach; to Mishael, Meshach; and to Azariah, Abednego.

But Daniel resolved not to defile himself with the royal food and wine, and he asked the chief official for

permission not to defile himself this way. Now God had caused the official to show favor and sympathy to Daniel, but the official told Daniel, "I am afraid of my lord the king, who has assigned your food and drink. Why should he see you looking worse than the other young men your age? The king would then have my head because of you."

But Daniel had a plan.

📖 "Please test your servants for ten days: Give us nothing but vegetables to eat and water to drink. Then compare our appearance with that of the young men who eat the royal food, and treat your servants in accordance with what you see." So he agreed to this and tested them for ten days.

At the end of the ten days they looked healthier and better nourished than any of the young men who ate the royal food. So the guard took away their choice food and the wine they were to drink and gave them vegetables instead.

To these four young men God gave knowledge and understanding of all kinds of literature and learning. And Daniel could understand visions and dreams of all kinds.

Daniel and his three friends were found to be the smartest and strongest. They were chosen to serve in the king's court.

■ Memory Verse:

Titus 2:11,12
For the grace of God that brings salvation has appeared to all men. It teaches us to say "No" to ungodliness and worldly passions, and to live self-controlled, upright and godly lives in this present age.

■ Character Trait:

Dedication—complete commitment to something or someone. When you are dedicated to someone, your whole heart is in what you are doing. Dedication may also involve the setting apart of something or someone for a special purpose.

■ Daniel 3:4-6, 16-18, 22, 23, 28-29

Me Bow? Nohow!

Nebuchadnezzar was a powerful king who was impressed with himself. He had workmen build a huge statue of a false god to represent the power and might of Babylon.

📖 Then the herald loudly proclaimed, "This is what you are **commanded to do, O peoples, nations and men of every language: As soon as you hear the sound of the horn, flute, zither, lyre, harp, pipes and all kinds of music, you must fall down and worship the image of gold that King Nebuchadnezzar has set up. Whoever does** not fall down and worship will immediately be thrown into a blazing furnace."

But Shadrach, Meshach, and Abednego did not bow. They were brought before the king.

📖 Shadrach, Meshach and Abednego replied to the king, "O Nebuchadnezzar, we do not need to defend ourselves before you in this matter. If we are thrown into the blazing furnace, the God we serve is able to save us from it, and he will rescue us from your hand, O king. But even if he does not, we want you to know, O king, that we will not serve your gods or worship the image of gold you have set up."

Then the king commanded that Shadrach, Meshach, and Abednego be thrown into a fiery furnace that had been heated seven times hotter than usual.

📖 The king's command was so urgent and the furnace so hot that the flames of the fire killed the soldiers who took up Shadrach, Meshach and Abednego, and these three men, firmly tied, fell into the blazing furnace.

But the king watched as a fourth man appeared in the furnace. All four men were unharmed and unbound. He commanded Shadrach, Meshach, and Abednego to come out.

📖 Then Nebuchadnezzar said, "Praise be to the God of Shadrach, Meshach and Abednego, who has sent his angel and rescued his servants! They trusted in him and defied the king's command and were willing to give up their lives rather than serve or worship any god except their own God. Therefore I decree that the people of any nation or language who say anything against the God of Shadrach, Meshach and Abednego be cut into pieces and their houses be turned into piles of rubble, for no other god can save in this way."

■ Memory Verse:

Psalm 19:14
May the words of my mouth and the meditation of my heart be pleasing in your sight, O Lord, my Rock and my Redeemer.

■ Character Trait:

Dedication—complete commitment to something or someone. Shadrach, Meshach, and Abednego were totally committed to serving God. They were dedicated to him.

Mysterious Message

Outside the walls of Babylon the Persian army waited for traitors within the city to open the gates. Inside the banquet hall of the palace, King Belshazzar ate and had a drunken party with his guests. But suddenly something terrifying happened.

📖 **Suddenly the fingers of a human hand appeared and wrote on the plaster of the wall, near the lampstand in the royal palace. The king watched the hand as it wrote.**

The king was frightened and sent for the magicians and astrologers. But none of them could read the handwriting on the wall.

📖 **So Daniel was brought before the king, the king said to him, "Are you Daniel, one of the exiles my father the king brought from Judah? I have heard that the spirit of the gods is in you and that you have insight, intelligence and outstanding wisdom. The wise men and enchanters were brought before me to read this writing and tell me what it means, but they could not explain it."**

Daniel was offered many gifts if he could tell what the handwriting meant.

📖 **Instead, you have set yourself up against the LORD of heaven. You**

had the goblets from his temple brought to you, and you and your nobles, your wives and your concubines drank wine from them. You praised the gods of silver and gold, of bronze, iron, wood and stone, which cannot see or hear or understand. But you did not honor the God who holds in his hand your life and all your ways. Therefore he sent the hand that wrote the inscription.

This is the inscription that was written: MENE, MENE, TEKEL, PARSIN This is what these words mean:

Mene: God has numbered the days of your reign and brought it to an end.

Tekel: You have been weighed on the scales and found wanting.

Peres: Your kingdom is divided and given to the Medes and Persians.

Then at Belshazzar's command, Daniel was clothed in purple, a gold chain was placed around his neck, and he was proclaimed the third highest ruler in the kingdom.

That night Daniel's prediction came true, and Darius the Mede, conquered Babylon.

■ Memory Verse:

I Timothy 2:1, 2

I urge, then, first of all, that requests, prayers, intercession and thanksgiving be made for everyone—for kings and all those in authority, that we may live peaceful and quiet lives in all godliness and holiness.

■ Character Trait:

Confidence—a feeling of security based on faith and trust. It is the firm belief that God can see you safely through any situation, no matter what the circumstances are.

Conspiracy

King Darius thought Daniel was unusually wise and often asked him for advice. Daniel's coworkers were jealous of him. Knowing that Daniel knelt and prayed to God, they asked King Darius to make a law.

□ So the administrators and the satraps went as a group to the king and said: "O King Darius, live forever! The royal administrators, prefects, satraps, advisers and governors have all agreed that the

king should issue an edict and enforce the decree that anyone who prays to any god or man during the next thirty days, except to you, O king, shall be thrown into the lions' den. Now, O king, issue the decree and put it in writing so that it cannot be altered—in accordance with the laws of the Medes and Persians, which cannot be repealed." So King Darius put the decree in writing.

Now when Daniel learned that the decree had been published, he went home to his upstairs room where the windows opened toward Jerusalem. Three times a day he got down on his knees and prayed, giving thanks to his God, just as he had done before.

The king tried to think of a way to save Daniel, but he could not disobey the law. So Daniel was thrown into the den of lions.

📖 A stone was brought and placed over the mouth of the den, and the king sealed it with his own signet ring and with the rings of his nobles, so that Daniel's situation might not be changed.

But the king refused his dinner and could not sleep. Early the next morning, he rushed to the lions' den, and called to Daniel.

📖 Daniel answered, "O king, live forever! My God sent his angel, and he shut the mouths of the lions. They have not hurt me, because I was found innocent in his sight. Nor have I ever done any wrong before you, O king."

The king was overjoyed and gave orders to lift Daniel out of the den. And when Daniel was lifted from the den, no wound was found on him, because he had trusted in his God.

At the king's command, the men who had falsely accused Daniel were brought in and thrown into the lions' den, along with their wives and children. And before they reached the floor of the den, the lions overpowered them and crushed all their bones.

So the king made a decree that everyone in the kingdom must worship the God of Daniel.

■ Memory Verse:

Psalm 16:8
I have set the Lord always before me. Because he is at my right hand, I will not be shaken.

■ Character Trait:

Conviction—a strong belief in or desire to uphold a moral standard. Your personal convictions are the things you believe to be right or wrong. As a result, they mold your thoughts and actions.

Going Fishing

God told Jonah to go to Nineveh, one of the most wicked cities in the world, with a message to repent or God would deliver the city to its enemies. Jonah was afraid to go, and sailed for Tarshish to flee from the Lord.

▢ Then the LORD sent a great wind on the sea, and such a violent storm arose that the ship threatened to break up. All the sailors were afraid and each cried out to his own god. And they threw the cargo into the sea to lighten the ship. But Jonah had gone below deck, where he lay down and fell into a deep sleep. The captain went to him and said, "How can you sleep? Get up and call on your god! Maybe he will take notice of us, and we will not perish." Then the sailors said to each other, "Come, let us cast lots to find out who is responsible for this calamity." They cast lots and the lot fell on Jonah.

Jonah told the sailors to throw him into the sea. Finally, the men did as Jonah asked.

▢ But the LORD provided a great fish to swallow Jonah, and Jonah was inside the fish three days and three nights. From inside the fish Jonah prayed to the LORD his God. He said: "In my distress I called to the LORD, and he answered me. From the depths of the grave I called for help, and you listened to my cry. You hurled me into the deep, into the very heart of the seas, and the currents swirled about me; all your waves and breakers swept over me. I said, 'I have been banished from your sight; yet I will look again toward your holy temple.' The engulfing waters threatened me, the deep surrounded me; seaweed was wrapped around my head. To the roots of the mountains I sank down; the earth beneath barred me in forever. But you brought my life up from the pit, O LORD my God.

"When my life was ebbing away, I remembered you, LORD, and my prayer rose to you, to your holy temple. "Those who cling to worthless idols forfeit the grace that could be theirs. But I, with a song of thanksgiving, will sac-

rifice to you. What I have vowed I will make good. Salvation comes from the Lord."
And the Lord commanded the fish, and it vomited Jonah onto dry land.

So, once again, God commanded Jonah to go to Nineveh. Jonah went and the city repented.

■ Memory Verse:
Matthew 22:39b
"...Love your neighbor as yourself."

■ Character Trait:
Obedience—doing what you are told to do. We are commanded to be obedient to God in every way. Obedience is part of our faith because it shows we know that God can teach

New Testament

A King Is Born

The details of Jesus' birth are miraculous. An angel told his mother, Mary, she was to have a child through the Holy Spirit. Mary was engaged to Joseph. But since they were not yet married, and Mary was pregnant, Joseph was troubled.

▢ Because Joseph her husband was a righteous man and did not want to expose her to public disgrace, he had in mind to divorce her quietly.

Then an angel came to Joseph in a dream to explain that the baby Mary was carrying was of the Holy Spirit and would be the Son of God.

▢ But after he had considered this, an angel of the LORD appeared to him in a dream and said, "Joseph son of David, do not be afraid to take Mary home as your wife, because what is conceived in her is from the Holy Spirit. She will give birth to a son, and you are to give him the name Jesus, because he will save his people from their sins." All this took place to fulfill what the LORD had said through the prophet: "The virgin will be with child and will give birth to a son, and they will call him Immanuel"—which means, "God with us."
When Joseph woke up, he did what the angel of the LORD had commanded him and took Mary home as his wife. But he had no union with her until she gave birth to a son. And he gave him the name Jesus.

So Joseph and Mary were married and Jesus was born.

■ **Memory Verse:**

Matthew 1:21
She will give birth to a son, and you are
to give him the name Jesus, because
he will save his people from their sins.

■ **Character Trait:**

Faith—the act of believing the things
that God has revealed about Himself
and acting on those beliefs. By faith
Mary and Joseph believed what the
angel of the Lord had told them.

Special Delivery

One night a large, brilliant star appeared in the east. The wise men decided to follow the star. They knew the star would lead them to Jesus. When they reached Jerusalem, they stopped to see King Herod, hoping that he knew where the baby was. Herod did not, but sent the wise men to Bethlehem.

📖 **He sent them to Bethlehem and said, "Go and make a careful search for the child. As soon as you find him, report to me, so that I too may go and worship him."**
After they had heard the king, they went on their way, and the star they had seen in the east went ahead of them until it stopped over the place

■ **Memory Verse:**

Luke 2:11
Today in the town of David a Savior has been born to you; he is Christ the Lord.

■ **Character Trait:**

Worship—to honor and adore someone who is worthy of high honor. True worship involves not only things we do, but also our thoughts and feelings as we do them. Only God fully deserves our worship, and we are to worship him both publicly and privately.

where the child was. When they saw the star, they were overjoyed. On coming to the house, they saw the child with his mother Mary, and they bowed down and worshiped him. Then they opened their treasures and presented him with gifts of gold and of incense and of myrrh.

An angel warned the wise men in a dream not to return to Herod, so they went home another way.

Protection Plan

King Herod planned to kill the baby Jesus. Joseph and Mary fled with the child to Egypt.

📖 When they had gone, an angel of the Lord appeared to Joseph in a dream. "Get up," he said, "take the child and his mother and escape to Egypt. Stay there until I tell you, for Herod is going to search for the child to kill him."
So he got up, took the child and his mother during the night and left for Egypt, where he stayed until the death of Herod. And so was fulfilled what the Lord had said through the prophet: "Out of Egypt I called my son."
When Herod realized that he had been outwitted by the Magi, he was furious, and he gave orders to kill all the boys in Bethlehem and its vicinity who were two years old and under, in accordance with the time

he had learned from the Magi.

After Herod died, an angel appeared to Joseph in Egypt and told him to take Mary and Joseph to Israel.

📖 **So he got up, took the child and his mother and went to the land of Israel. But when he heard that Archelaus was reigning in Judea in place of his father Herod, he was afraid to go there. Having been warned in a dream, he withdrew to the district of Galilee, and he went and lived in a town called Nazareth. So was fulfilled what was said through the prophets: "He will be called a Nazarene."**

■ **Memory Verse:**
Romans 8:31
What, then, shall we say in response to this? If God is for us, who can be against us?

■ **Character Trait:**
Confidence—a feeling of security based on faith and trust. It is the firm belief that God can see you safely through any situation. Real confidence is based on God's ability to take care of you.

Faithful in Forgiveness

The famous "eye for eye, tooth for tooth" is found in Jewish law (Exodus. 21:24). In general, Jewish rabbis taught that it was reasonable to forgive your brother seven times; after that, he could be considered an enemy. Jesus' lesson on forgiveness went further.

📖 Then Peter came to Jesus and asked, "Lord, how many times shall I forgive my brother when he sins against me? Up to seven times?"
Jesus answered, "I tell you, not seven times, but seventy-seven times.
"Therefore, the kingdom of heaven is like a king who wanted to settle accounts with his servants. As he began the settlement, a man who owed him ten thousand talents was brought to him. Since he was not able to pay, the master ordered that he and his wife and his children and all that he had be sold to repay the debt.

"The servant fell on his knees before him. 'Be patient with me,' he begged, 'and I will pay back everything.' The servant's master took pity on him, canceled the debt and let him go.

But when the man left the king, he found someone who owed him money

and refused to forgive the man his debt. The creditor had the man arrested.

📖 **When the other servants saw what had happened, they were greatly distressed and went and told their master everything that had happened.**

In anger his master turned him over to the jailers until he should pay back all he owed.

Jesus said God would not forgive our sins if we did not forgive others.

■ Memory Verse:

Psalm 66:18
If I had cherished sin in my heart, the Lord would not have listened.

■ Character Trait:

Forgiveness—forgetting or blotting out someone's sin or guilt. Any request for forgiveness should go with a desire to make up for the wrong. It was not easy for Jesus to die on the cross so God could forgive us. Sometimes it is difficult to forgive others, but to forgive is always the right thing to do.

Generation Gap

Each spring Mary, Joseph, and Jesus attended the Passover Feast in Jerusalem. As twelve-year-old Jesus worshiped in the temple, He thought of many questions to ask the teachers of the Jews. But when the feast was over, the people began their journey home. Jesus remained in the temple, but Mary and Joseph did not know it.

📖 **Thinking he was in their company, they traveled on for a day. Then they began looking for him among their relatives and friends. When they did not find him, they went back to Jerusalem to look for him. After three days they found him in the temple courts, sitting among the teach-**

■ Memory Verse:

Proverbs 1:8
Listen, my son, to your father's instruction and do not forsake your
mother's teaching.

■ Character Trait:

Concern—a feeling of anxiety about
or interest in someone else. Showing
concern indicates that you care
enough about someone to think about
that person and to act on his or her
behalf.

ers, listening to them and asking them questions. Everyone who heard him was amazed at his understanding and his answers. When his parents saw him, they were astonished. His mother said to him, "Son, why have you treated us like this? Your father and I have been anxiously searching for you."

"Why were you searching for me?" he asked. "Didn't you know I had to be in my Father's house?"

Changed by Faith

Nicodemus was a Pharisee and a member of the Sanhedrin, the highest Jewish assembly for the government. He felt lonely inside and was searching for something more. Nicodemus did not want to offend the Pharisees by approaching Jesus in the daytime. So he went to see Jesus at night.

📖 In reply Jesus declared, "I tell you the truth, no one can see the kingdom of God unless he is born again."

"How can a man be born when he is old?" Nicodemus asked. "Surely he cannot enter a second time into his mother's womb to be born!"

Jesus answered, "I tell you the truth, no one can enter the kingdom of God unless he is born of water and the Spirit. Flesh gives birth to flesh, but the Spirit gives birth to spirit. You should not be surprised at my saying, 'You must be born again.'

■ **Memory Verse:**

John 3:16
For God so loved the world that he gave his one and only Son, that whoever believes in him shall not perish but have eternal life.

■ **Character Trait:**

Initiative—the readiness to take needed action without waiting around for someone else to act. Most people are able to look around and see many things that need to be done. Initiative goes beyond observing and talking about those things, into actually getting something accomplished.

But Nicodemus was still puzzled. So Jesus explained further.

📖 **"Just as Moses lifted up the snake in the desert, so the Son of Man must be lifted up, that everyone who believes in him may have eternal life. For God so loved the world that he gave his one and only Son, that whoever believes in him shall not perish but have eternal life.**

For God did not send his Son into the world to condemn the world, but to save the world through him. Whoever believes in him is not condemned, but whoever does not believe stands condemned already because he has not believed in the name of God's one and only Son."

Jesus gave Nicodemus a lot to think about. Their conversation ended, but Nicodemus did not forget Jesus.

Teach Us to Pray

Jesus had been praying. When He finished, one of the disciples asked, "Lord, teach us to pray."

📖 This, then, is how you should pray: "Our Father in heaven, hallowed be your name, your kingdom come, your will be done on earth as it is in heaven. Give us today our daily bread. Forgive us our debts, as we also have forgiven our debtors. And lead us not into temptation, but deliver us from the evil one." For if you forgive men when they sin against you, your heavenly Father will also forgive you.

Though the disciples used different words when they prayed, they used this prayer as an example of how to pray.

■ Memory Verse:

Mark 11:24

Therefore I tell you, whatever you ask for in prayer, believe that you have received it, and it will be yours.

■ Character Trait:

Prayerfulness—the regular act of praying. It includes much more than asking God for things you want. Prayer includes praising God, giving thanks for His blessings, confessing your sins, asking Him for help, and praying for other people.

Two Kinds of Bread

The crowd that followed Jesus was hungry. The only food that was available, five barley loaves and two fishes, belonged to a boy. The boy gave his food to Jesus, who thanked God for it and handed it to His disciples to distribute to the people.

Jesus then took the loaves, gave thanks, and distributed to those who were seated as much as they wanted. He did the same with the fish.
When they had all had enough to eat, he said to his disciples, "Gather the pieces that are left over. Let nothing be wasted."

The people were filled, and 12 baskets of food were left over.

■ Memory Verse:

John 6:47, 48
I tell you the truth, he who believes has everlasting life. I am the bread of life.

■ Character Trait:

Unselfishness—thinking of others before yourself. An unselfish person does not get caught up in his own problems while neglecting others. While it is okay to make sure your life goes smoothly, it is wrong to live as if you are the only one whose feelings matter.

Two Kinds of Blindness

Jesus and his disciples found a blind man begging at the temple gate. Jesus moistened some clay and gently placed it on the man's eyes.

📖 "Go," he told him, "wash in the Pool of Siloam." So the man went and washed, and came home seeing. His neighbors and those who had formerly seen him begging asked, "Isn't this the same man who used to sit and beg?" Some claimed that he was. Others said, "No, he only looks like him." But he himself insisted, "I am the man." "How then were your eyes opened?" they demanded. He replied, "The man they call Jesus made some mud and put it on my eyes. He told me to go to Siloam and wash. So I went and washed, and then I could see."

The Pharisees tried to make the man turn against Jesus, but they could not. So they threw the man out of the synagogue. Jesus knew what the Pharisees had tried to do and searched for the man.

📖 Jesus heard that they had thrown him out, and when he found him, he said, "Do you believe in the Son of Man?" "Who is he, sir?" the man asked. "Tell me so that I may believe in him." Jesus said, "You have now seen him; in fact, he is the one speaking with you." Then the man said, "Lord, I believe," and he worshiped him.

Jesus told the Pharisees they were guilty of a different kind of blindness. Their eyes could see, but they were spiritually blind and did not believe what Jesus taught them.

■ **Memory Verse:**
John 8:12
When Jesus spoke again to the people, he said, "I am the light of the world. Whoever follows me will never walk in darkness, but will have the light of life."

■ **Character Trait:**
Confidence—a feeling of security based on faith and trust. It is the firm belief that God can see you safely through any situation. You can have confidence in yourself or in others, but real confidence is based on God's ability to care for you.

Manhunt

A large group of people gathered to hear Jesus speak. He told them about a shepherd who had 100 sheep and lost one in the wilderness. The shepherd searched until the lost sheep was finally found.

▭ And when he finds it, he joyfully puts it on his shoulders and goes home. Then he calls his friends and neighbors together and says, "Rejoice with me; I have found my lost sheep." I tell you that in the same way there will be more rejoicing in heaven over one sinner who repents than over ninety-nine righteous persons who do not need to repent.

■ **Memory Verse:**
John 10:27
My sheep listen to my voice; I know them, and they follow me.

■ **Character Trait:**
Joyfulness—an intense feeling of good. In the Bible, it usually is associated with God's triumph over evil. A joyful person feels right about his relationships to God, to himself, and to others. Joyfulness is an inner gladness that can exist no matter what happens. It does not depend on outside circumstances.

Home for Good

Jesus told the Pharisees about a young man who demanded his inheritance and left home. He wasted his money, and at last had to take care of a farmer's pigs so he could eat. In his misery he went home to work for his father—as a servant. But his father had other plans.

📖 So he got up and went to his father.

"But while he was still a long way off, his father saw him and was filled with compassion for him; he ran to his son, threw his arms around him and kissed him."

"The son said to him, 'Father, I have sinned against heaven and against you. I am no longer worthy to be called your son.'"

"But the father said to his servants, 'Quick! Bring the best robe and put it on him. Put a ring on his finger and sandals on his feet. Bring the fattened calf and kill it. Let's have a feast and celebrate. For this son of mine was dead and is alive again; he was lost and is found.' So they began to celebrate."

At first the older brother, who had faithfully served his father, was jealous of the celebration. But his father explained.

📖 "But we had to celebrate and be glad, because this brother of yours was dead and is alive again; he was lost and is found."

■ Memory Verse:

Numbers 14:18a
The Lord is slow to anger, abounding in love and forgiving sin and rebellion.

■ Character Trait:

Repentance—sorrow for one's sin, and turning away from that sin to serve God and do right. Whenever you turn away from sin, you turn back toward God. When you feel genuine sorrow and ask God to forgive you for the things you've done wrong, you are repenting.

Surprise Ending

Lazarus, the brother of Mary and Martha, and a dear friend of Jesus, was sick. By the time Jesus and His disciples reached Bethany, where Lazarus lived, he had been dead for four days. Jesus ordered Lazarus' tombstone rolled away.

📖 **So they took away the stone. Then Jesus looked up and said, "Father, I thank you that you have heard me. I knew that you always hear me, but I said this for the benefit of the people standing here, that they may believe that you sent me." When he had said this, Jesus called in a loud voice, "Lazarus, come out!" The dead man came out, his hands and feet wrapped with strips of linen, and a cloth around his face.**
Jesus said to them, "Take off the grave clothes and let him go."

Many believed in Jesus after they saw Lazarus raised from the dead.

■ **Memory Verse:**
John 11:25
Jesus said to her, "I am the resurrection and the life. He who believes in me will live, even though he dies."

■ **Character Trait:**
Faith—the act of believing the things that God has revealed about himself and acting on those beliefs. It is the confident assurance that something we want is going to happen. It is the certainty that what we hope for is waiting for us, even though we cannot see it up ahead. People who are Christians are to live by faith.

114

Something Is Missing

One day a rich young ruler came to Jesus and knelt on the dusty road. He asked Jesus how to inherit eternal life.

📖 Now a man came up to Jesus and asked, "Teacher, what good thing must I do to get eternal life?"

"Why do you ask me about what is good?" Jesus replied. "There is only One who is good. If you want to enter life, obey the command- ments."

"Which ones?" the man inquired. Jesus replied, " 'Do not murder, do

116

■ **Memory Verse:**

Mark 12:30
Love the Lord your God with all your heart and with all your soul and with all your mind and with all your strength.

■ **Character Trait:**

Commitment—a willingness to serve someone or a cause. It involves your mental and physical loyalties to that person or purpose. A commitment should be taken seriously, especially where your relationship with God is concerned.

not commit adultery, do not steal, do not give false testimony, honor your father and mother,' and 'love your neighbor as yourself.' "
"All these I have kept," the young man said. "What do I still lack?"
Jesus answered, "If you want to be perfect, go, sell your possessions and give to the poor, and you will have treasure in heaven. Then come, follow me."

The young man went away sad because he had great wealth. Jesus said it was very hard for a rich man to enter the kingdom of heaven.

Who's the Boss?

People in Jesus' day traveled mainly by walking on the hot, dusty roads of Israel. After a long journey, their feet were tired and dirty. Servants washed the feet of the travelers with cool water. Jesus began to wash the feet of His disciples. But Peter had other plans.

 "No," said Peter, "you shall never wash my feet."
Jesus answered, "Unless I wash you, you have no part with me."
"Then, Lord," Simon Peter replied, "not just my feet but my hands and my head as well!"
Jesus answered, "A person who has had a bath needs only to wash his feet; his whole body is clean. And you are clean, though not every one of you."

Jesus knew Judas would betray Him, and that is why He said not everyone was clean.

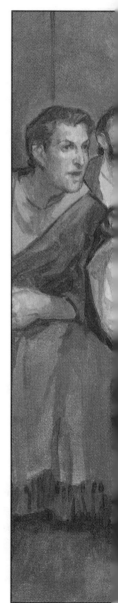

■ Memory Verse:
I Corinthians 6:14
By his power God raised the Lord from the dead, and he will raise us also.

■ Character Trait:
Humility—the voluntary lowering of yourself or the willingness to give up something that should rightfully be yours. To be humble, you must eliminate pride and arrogance. A humble person is not weak. It takes great inner strength to allow someone to take credit for something you have done and not to boast about yourself.

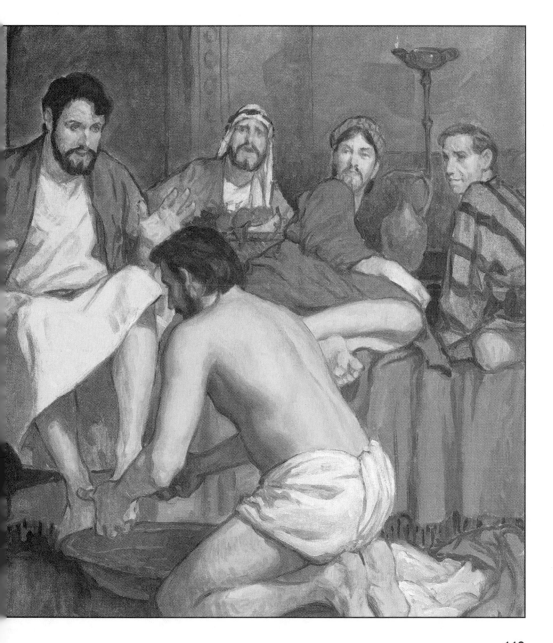

The Fruit Jesus Likes Best

Grapevines need much care. Each spring they must be pruned and the dead branches burned. Jesus used this as a word picture of how God helps each Christian to become a better person.

 I am the true vine, and my Father is the gardener. He cuts off every branch in me that bears no fruit, while every branch that does bear fruit he prunes so that it will be even more fruitful. You are already clean because of the word I have spoken to you. Remain in me, and I will remain in you. No branch can bear fruit by itself; it must remain in the vine. Neither can you bear fruit unless you remain in me.

I am the vine; you are the branches. If a man remains in me and I in him, he will bear much fruit; apart from me you can do nothing. If anyone does not remain in me, he is like a branch that is thrown away and withers; such branches are picked up, thrown into the fire and burned. If you remain in me and my words remain in you, ask whatever you wish, and it will be given you. This is to my Father's glory, that you bear much fruit, showing yourselves to be my disciples.

Jesus told His disciples that others would know they were His followers by the way they acted.

■ Memory Verse:

John 15:5a
I am the vine; you are the branches. If a man remains in me and I in him, he will bear much fruit.

■ Character Trait:

Faithfulness—in one sense, a synonym for loyalty. But from a biblical perspective, it is possible to be loyal without being faithful. Faithfulness suggests being "full of faith," so it is a measure of your relationship with God.

Betrayal

Judas may have started out as a loyal follower, but he became greedy. At the Last Supper, Jesus warned His disciples that Judas would betray Him. And while Jesus was in the Garden of Gethsemane, Judas came with soldiers to betray Him.

📖 **Then he returned to the disciples and said to them, "Are you still sleeping and resting? Look, the hour is near, and the Son of Man is betrayed into the hands of sinners. Rise, let us go! Here comes my betrayer!"**
While he was still speaking, Judas, one of the Twelve, arrived. With him was a large crowd armed with swords and clubs, sent from the chief priests and the elders of the people. Now the betrayer had arranged a signal with them: "The one I kiss is the man; arrest him." Going at once to Jesus, Judas said, "Greetings, Rabbi!" and kissed him.

One of Jesus' disciples cut off the ear of the servant of the high priest. Jesus healed the servant's ear. All the disciples deserted Jesus and fled.

📖 **Those who had arrested Jesus took him to Caiaphas, the high priest, where the teachers of the law and the elders had assembled.**

The chief priests and the Sanhedrin searched for false evidence against Jesus so they could kill him.

📖 **But Jesus remained silent.**
The high priest said to him, "I charge you under oath by the living God: Tell us if you are the Christ, the Son of God."
"Yes, it is as you say," Jesus replied. "But I say to all of you: In the future you will see the Son of Man sitting at the right hand of the Mighty One and coming on the clouds of heaven."
Then the high priest tore his clothes and said, "He has spoken blasphemy! Why do we need any more witnesses? Look, now you have heard the blasphemy. What do you think?"
"He is worthy of death," they answered.
Then they spit in his face and struck him with their fists.

■ Memory Verse:

Matthew 26:41
Watch and pray so that you will not fall into temptation. The spirit is willing, but the body is weak.

■ Character Trait:

Perseverance—the ability to keep going under pressure without being discouraged.

Before and After

While Jesus was on trial, Peter, who secretly followed Jesus into the city, warmed his hands by a fire in the palace courtyard. While he was talking, a maid stared at him.

📖 **Now Peter was sitting out in the courtyard, and a servant girl came to him. "You also were with Jesus of Galilee," she said. But he denied it before them all. "I don't know what you're talking**

■ **Memory Verse:**

Isaiah 41:10b
I will strengthen you and help you;
I will uphold you with my righteous
right hand.

■ **Character Trait:**

Loyalty—a strong devotion to a person or ideal. True loyalty is a willingness to stand by your friends and your beliefs even if it is unpopular to do so.

about," he said.

Then he went out to the gateway, where another girl saw him and said to the people there, "This fellow was with Jesus of Nazareth." He denied it again, with an oath: "I don't know the man!"

After a little while, those standing there went up to Peter and said, "Surely you are one of them, for your accent gives you away."

Then he began to call down curses on himself and he swore to them, "I don't know the man!"

Immediately a rooster crowed.

Then Peter remembered Jesus' warning that he would deny Jesus three times. Peter walked out of the courtyard and began to cry.

Pilate Washes His Hands

Jesus was taken before Pilate, the governor. Pilate was trapped. He didn't believe Jesus was guilty of treason. But he knew the Jewish leaders would make trouble if he let Jesus go. Then the Emperor in Rome would hold Pilate responsible.

Now it was the governor's custom at the Feast to release a prisoner chosen by the crowd.
But the chief priests and the elders persuaded the crowd to ask for Barabbas and to have Jesus executed.
"Which of the two do you want me to release to you?" asked the governor.
"Barabbas," they answered.
"What shall I do, then, with Jesus who is called Christ?" Pilate asked.
They all answered, "Crucify him!"
"Why? What crime has he committed?" asked Pilate.
But they shouted all the louder, "Crucify him!"
When Pilate saw that he was getting nowhere, but that instead an uproar was starting, he took water and

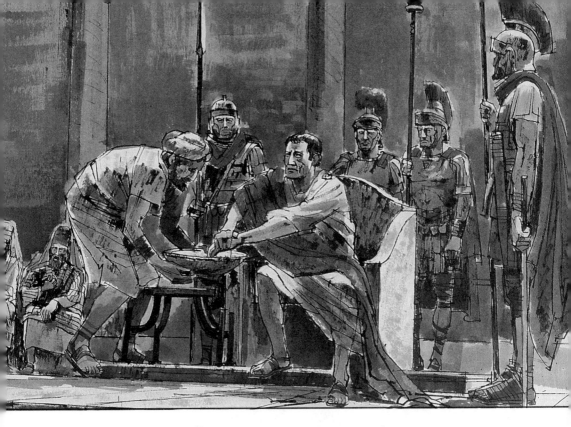

washed his hands in front of the crowd. "I am innocent of this man's blood," he said. "It is your responsibility!"
All the people answered, "Let his blood be on us and on our children!"
Then he released Barabbas to them. But he had Jesus flogged, and handed him over to be crucified.

So Jesus was crucified.

📖 When they had crucified him, they divided up his clothes by casting lots. And sitting down, they kept watch over him there. Above his head they placed the written charge against him: THIS IS JESUS, THE KING OF THE JEWS. Two robbers were crucified with him, one on his right and one on his left.

A friend of Jesus, Joseph of Arimathea, asked for Jesus' body, and Pilate gave it to him.

■ Memory verse:
Hebrews 9:22b
And without the shedding of blood there is no forgiveness.

■ Character Trait:
Forgiveness—blotting out sin and guilt. There is no way we can make up to God for our sins. Pilate could not wash his guilt away for condemning Jesus. Jesus died on the cross so we can be forgiven of the things we do wrong.

The Great Mystery

The chief priests and the Pharisees asked Pilate to place a guard at the tomb. So a guard was placed at the tomb and a Roman seal was placed over the stone. But Jesus did not stay in the tomb.

📖 After the Sabbath, at dawn on the first day of the week, Mary Magdalene and the other Mary went to look at the tomb.
There was a violent earthquake, for an angel of the Lord came down from heaven and, going to the tomb, rolled back the stone and sat on it. His appearance was like lightning, and his clothes were white as snow. The guards were so afraid of him

■ **Memory Verse:**

II Corinthians 5:21
God made him who had no sin to be sin for us, so that in him we might become the righteousness of God.

■ **Character Trait:**

Faith—the act of believing the things God has revealed about himself and acting on those beliefs. The women believed the angel even though they had not seen Jesus yet.

that they shook and became like dead men.

The angel said to the women, "Do not be afraid, for I know that you are looking for Jesus, who was crucified. He is not here; he has risen, just as he said. Come and see the place where he lay. Then go quickly and tell his disciples: 'He has risen from the dead and is going ahead of you into Galilee. There you will see him.' Now I have told you."

So the women ran to tell the disciples that Jesus had risen.

The Confrontation

After Jesus' resurrection, the disciples met behind locked doors because they feared arrest. Jesus appeared to them. At first, Thomas did not believe Jesus had risen.

📖 **They were startled and frightened, thinking they saw a ghost. He said to them, "Why are you troubled, and why do doubts rise in your minds? Look at my hands and my feet. It is I myself! Touch me and see; a ghost does not have flesh and bones, as you see I have." When he had said this, he showed them his hands and feet.**

The disciples were shocked, and Jesus helped them understand that the Scriptures said He would die and rise again on the third day.

■ Memory Verse:

John 20:31
But these are written that you may believe that Jesus is the Christ, the Son of God, and that by believing you may have life in his name.

■ Character Trait:

Faith—the act of believing the things that God has revealed about Himself and acting on those beliefs. It is the certainty that what we hope for is waiting for us, even though we cannot see it up ahead. People who are Christians live by faith.

From Fisherman to Shepherd

After denying Jesus, Peter felt like a failure. The disciples knew they would have to stick together and went fishing. They fished all night and caught nothing.

Early in the morning, Jesus stood on the shore, but the disciples did not realize that it was Jesus.
He called out to them, "Friends, haven't you any fish?"
"No," they answered. He said, "Throw your net on the right side of the boat and you will find some." When they did, they were unable to haul the net in because of the large number of fish. Then the disciple whom Jesus loved said to Peter, "It is the Lord!" As soon as Simon Peter heard him say, "It is the Lord," he wrapped his outer garment around him (for he had taken it off) and jumped into the water.

The disciples came to the shore and ate breakfast with Jesus.

When they had finished eating, Jesus said to Simon Peter, "Simon son of John, do you truly love me more than these?"
"Yes, LORD, " he said, "you know that I love you."
Jesus said, "Feed my lambs."

■ Memory Verse:

Hebrews 10:24
And let us consider how we may spur one another on toward love and good deeds.

■ Character Trait:

Loyalty—a strong devotion to a person or ideal. True loyalty is a willingness to stand by your friends and your beliefs when no one else is willing to do so. The disciples were loyal to each other. Later, they were so loyal to Jesus that they gave their lives preaching His gospel.

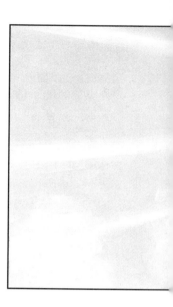

Together Forever

The 11 disciples returned to Jerusalem. Jesus told them that by His death and resurrection He had fulfilled God's mission for Him to be Savior of the world. He told them to carry on the work, but to wait for the Holy Spirit.

📖 **But you will receive power when the Holy Spirit comes on you; and you will be my witnesses in Jerusalem, and in all Judea and Samaria, and to the ends of the earth."**
After he said this, he was taken up before their very eyes, and a cloud hid him from their sight.
They were looking intently up into the sky as he was going, when suddenly two men dressed in white stood beside them. "Men of Galilee," they said, "why do you stand

■ Memory Verse:

John 14:1
Do not let your hearts be troubled.
Trust in God; trust also in me.

here looking into the sky? This same
Jesus, who has been taken from
you into heaven, will come back in
the same way you have seen him go
into heaven."

The disciples were amazed, but
stayed in Jerusalem to wait for the
coming of the Holy Spirit.

■ Character Trait:

Prayerfulness—the regular act of
praying. It involves much more than
asking God for things you want.
Prayer includes praising God, giving
thanks for His blessings, confessing
your sins, asking Him for help, and
praying for other people. Prayerfulness gives you a proper perspective
on life.

■ **Acts 2:1-4**

Transformed!

The disciples, who had once fled for fear of being arrested as friends of Jesus, returned to Jerusalem. They knew Jesus was depending on them to tell others all over the world about Him. Meanwhile, Jews from all over Palestine and distant countries gathered in Jerusalem to celebrate Pentecost.

▢ When the day of Pentecost came, they were all together in one place. Suddenly a sound like the blowing of a violent wind came from heaven and filled the whole house where they were sitting. They saw what seemed to be tongues of fire that separated and came to rest on each of them. All of them were filled with

the Holy Spirit and began to speak in other tongues as the Spirit enabled them.

The disciples were filled with strength and courage and began to preach—each in a different language. Thousands of people believed in Jesus and were baptized that day.

■ Memory Verse:

Philippians 2:13
For it is God who works in you to will and to act according to his good purpose.

■ Character Trait:

Purposefulness—the determination to complete whatever you set out to do. When God gives someone a job to do, that person should feel a sense of purpose as he or she tries to do what God has commanded.

Mixed Motives

Many of the believers shared their possessions. A warm fellowship existed among them. But Ananias and his wife Sapphira sold property and brought only a part of the money. They said they had brought the full price.

📖 Then Peter said, "Ananias, how is it that Satan has so filled your heart that you have lied to the Holy Spirit and have kept for yourself some of the money you received for the land? Didn't it belong to you before it was sold? And after it was sold, wasn't the money at your disposal? What made you think of doing such a thing? You have not lied to men but to God."

When Ananias heard this, he fell

down and died. And great fear seized all who heard what had happened. Then the young men came forward, wrapped up his body, and carried him out and buried him.

Later Sapphira came in, not knowing Ananias had been struck dead for his lie. She, too, lied.

📖 Peter said to her, "How could you agree to test the Spirit of the Lord? Look! The feet of the men who buried your husband are at the door, and they will carry you out also."
At that moment she fell down at his feet and died. Then the young men came in and, finding her dead, carried her out and buried her beside her husband.

Those who saw and heard what had happened to Ananias and Sapphira were filled with fear.

■ Memory Verse:

II Corinthians 9:7
Each man should give what he has decided in his heart to give, not reluctantly or under compulsion, for God loves a cheerful giver.

■ Character Trait:

Honesty—telling the truth and not being deceitful. It is possible to tell the truth with your words, yet by your actions deceive others. If you are honest, neither your words nor your actions will mislead anyone.

Saul's Rise and Fall and Rise

Stephen accused the Sanhedrin of not keeping God's laws. Then Stephen told them he saw Jesus standing at the right hand of God.

📖 **At this they covered their ears and, yelling at the top of their voices, they all rushed at him, dragged him out of the city and began to stone him. Meanwhile, the witnesses laid their clothes at the feet of a young man named Saul.**

Stephen prayed that the Lord would forgive them for stoning him, and then he died. Meanwhile, Saul of Tarsus watched Stephen's stoning and death. Saul hated Christians. He was on his way to Damascus to arrest Christians when his life was changed.

📖 **As he neared Damascus on his journey, suddenly a light from heaven flashed around him. He fell to the ground and heard a voice say**

to him, "Saul, Saul, why do you persecute me?"

"Who are you, Lord?" Saul asked.

"I am Jesus, whom you are persecuting," he replied. "Now get up and go into the city, and you will be told what you must do."

The men traveling with Saul stood there speechless; they heard the sound but did not see anyone. Saul got up from the ground, but when he opened his eyes he could see nothing. So they led him by the hand into Damascus. For three days he was blind, and did not eat or drink anything.

■ Memory Verse:

Ephesians 4:32
Be kind and compassionate to one another, forgiving each other, just as in Christ God forgave you.

■ Character Trait:

Repentance—sorrow for one's sin, and turning away from that sin to serve God and do right. If your sins include offenses against other people, make sure you repent to those people as well. Whenever you turn away from sin, you turn back toward God.

Ready, Set, Preach

God sent a Christian named Ananias to pray for Saul (later named Paul) and to heal his blindness. Saul stayed with the believers in Damascus for a few days. Then he went to the synagogue to preach. But the Sanhedrin planned to kill Saul.

📖 **But Saul learned of their plan. Day and night they kept close watch on the city gates in order to kill him. But his followers took him by night and lowered him in a basket through an opening in the wall.**

Saul escaped and traveled to Jerusalem.

■ Memory Verse:
Romans 12:1
Therefore, I urge you, brothers, in view of God's mercy, to offer your bodies as living sacrifices, holy and pleasing to God—this is your spiritual act of worship.

■ Character Trait:
Kindness—a sympathetic attitude and a willingness to be helpful whenever possible. Kindness begins with consideration for others and is demonstrated when specific needs arise.

Stronger Than Chains

Peter was arrested and put in prison. But the night before Herod planned to sentence Peter, an angel of God entered Peter's prison cell. He told Peter to get up and follow him.

📖 **Peter followed him out of the prison, but he had no idea that what the angel was doing was really happening; he thought he was seeing a vision. They passed the first and second guards and came to the iron gate leading to the city. It opened for them by itself, and they went through it. When they had walked the length of one street, suddenly the angel left him.**

Peter knew the Lord had sent His angel to free him from prison and save him from Herod's wrath. Peter went to Mary's house. A girl named Rhoda came to open the door.

📖 **When she recognized Peter's voice, she was so overjoyed she ran back without opening it and exclaimed, "Peter is at the door!"** "You're out of your mind," they told her. When she kept insisting that it was so, they said, "It must be his angel."

Peter continued knocking, and they finally let him in. He told them how the Lord had freed him from prison. Then Peter left for a safer place.

■ Memory Verse:

Matthew 7:7
Ask and it will be given to you; seek and you will find; knock and the door will be opened to you.

■ Character Trait:

Faith—believing what God has said about Himself and acting on those beliefs. Peter's friends prayed for his release, but were shocked when he landed on their doorstep. They knew God had the power to release Peter from prison, but did not believe that he would really be freed. They did not have faith.

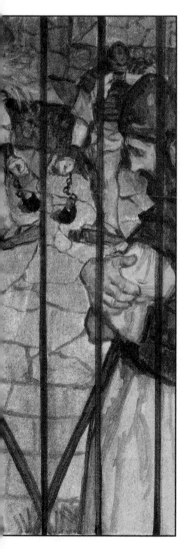

A Tale of Four Cities

Paul and Barnabas were forced to leave Antioch to escape persecution. They went southeast about 80 miles to Iconium, another city in the province of Galatia. There Jews and Greeks accepted the good news of Jesus. This angered the Jewish leaders.

📖 **There was a plot afoot among the Gentiles and Jews, together with their leaders, to mistreat them and stone them. But they found out about it and fled to the Lycaonian cities of Lystra and Derbe and to the surrounding country, where they continued to preach the good news.**

In Lystra, Paul healed a lame man. The people wanted to worship Paul and Barnabas. This upset Paul and Barnabas, who gave God the glory for the lame man's healing.

📖 **Men, why are you doing this? We too are only men, human like you. We are bringing you good news, telling you to turn from these worthless things to the living God, who made heaven and earth and sea and everything in them.**

But Paul and Barnabas' enemies from Iconium had followed them.

📖 **Then some Jews came from Antioch and Iconium and won the crowd over. They stoned Paul and dragged him outside the city, thinking he was dead. But after the disciples had gathered around him, he got up and went back into the city. The next day he and Barnabas left for Derbe.**

■ Memory Verse:

II Corinthians 1:21a
Now it is God who makes both us and you stand firm in Christ. He anointed us.

■ Character Trait:

Commitment—a willingness to serve someone or a cause. It involves your mental and physical loyalties to that person or purpose. A commitment should be taken seriously, especially where your relationship with God is concerned.

The Shake-up

Paul restored a young girl to her right mind. She was a fortuneteller for some greedy men. Angry because their businesses had been ruined, the men dragged Paul and Silas before judges. They were beaten and thrown in jail. Suddenly, the prison foundation shook. The walls cracked, chains snapped, and heavy doors flew open.

The jailer woke up, and when he saw the prison doors open, he drew his sword and was about to kill himself because he thought the prisoners had escaped. But Paul shouted, "Don't harm yourself! We are all here!"

The jailer called for lights, rushed in and fell trembling before Paul and Silas. He then brought them out and asked, "Sirs, what must I do to be saved?"

They replied, "Believe in the Lord Jesus, and you will be saved—you and your household." Then they spoke the word of the Lord to him and to all the others in his house. At that hour of the night the jailer took them and washed their wounds; then immediately he and all his family were baptized. The jailer brought them into his house and set a meal before them; he was filled with joy because he had come to believe in God—he and his whole family.

When it was daylight, the magistrates sent their officers to the jailer with the order: "Release those men." The jailer told Paul, "The magistrates have ordered that you and Silas be released. Now you can leave. Go in peace."

When the magistrates discovered that Paul and Silas were Roman citizens and that they had beaten and imprisoned Paul and Silas without a trial, they were alarmed. They went to the prison to apologize to Paul and Silas and to set them free.

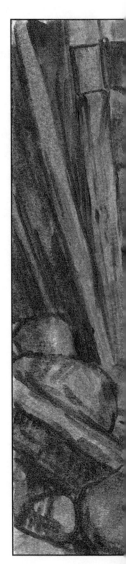

■ Memory Verse:

Acts 16:31
They replied, "Believe in the Lord Jesus, and you will be saved—you and your household."

■ Character Trait:

Compassion—a combination of love, care, and the desire to help. Sometimes the word pity is used for compassion. But true compassion goes beyond pity and includes a willingness to get involved in the problems of suffering people.

If at First
You Don't Succeed...

Paul and Silas traveled to Thessalonica where Paul preached at the synagogue. The Jews gathered a strong mob. Paul, Silas, and Timothy went to Berea. But their enemies followed them. Paul's friends helped him escape to Athens.

📖 **While Paul was waiting for them in Athens, he was greatly distressed to see that the city was full of idols. So he reasoned in the synagogue with the Jews and the God-fearing Greeks, as well as in the marketplace day by day with those who happened to be there. A group of Epicurean and Stoic philosophers began to dispute with him. Some of them asked, "What is this babbler trying to say?" Others remarked, "He seems to be advocating foreign gods." They said this because Paul was preaching the good news about Jesus and the resurrection. Then they took him and brought him to a meeting of the Areopagus, where they said to him, "May we know what this new teaching is that you are presenting? You are bringing some strange ideas to our ears, and we want to know what they mean."**

Paul preached to them. When Paul told them about the resurrection of Jesus, some sneered, but some wanted to hear more. A few became followers of Paul and believed on Jesus.

■ Memory Verse:

II Timothy 1:7
For God did not give us a spirit of timidity, but a spirit of power, of love and of self-discipline.

■ Character Trait:

Repentance—sorrow for one's sin and turning away from that sin to serve God and do right. Whenever you turn away from sin, you turn toward God. When you feel genuine sorrow and ask God to forgive you for the things you have done wrong, you are repenting.

No Turning Back

After spending nearly three years in Ephesus, Paul set out on his third and final missionary journey. He returned to churches he had visited on other trips. God told him to return to Jerusalem.

📖 **And now, compelled by the Spirit, I am going to Jerusalem, not knowing what will happen to me there. I only know that in every city the Holy Spirit warns me that prison and hardships are facing me. However, I consider my life worth nothing to me, if only I may finish the race and complete the task the Lord Jesus has given me—the task of testifying to the gospel of God's grace.**

A prophet warned Paul he would go to prison if he went to Jerusalem. Paul assured his friends he was ready for whatever faced him. He prayed with them and left for Jerusalem.

📖 **They all wept as they embraced him and kissed him.**

What grieved them most was his statement that they would never see his face again. Then they accompanied him to the ship.

■ **Memory Verse:**

Romans 8:28

And we know that in all things God works for the good of those who love him, who have been called according to his purpose.

■ **Character Trait:**

Dedication—complete commitment to something or someone. When you are dedicated to someone, your whole heart is in what you are doing. Dedication may also involve the setting apart of something or someone for a special purpose.

The Delayed Verdict

The Jews presented their charges against Paul to Felix, the Roman governor. Paul defended himself.

📖 **Several days later Felix came with his wife Drusilla, who was a Jewess. He sent for Paul and listened to him as he spoke about faith in Christ Jesus. As Paul discoursed on righteousness, self-control and the judgment to come, Felix was afraid and said, "That's enough for now! You may leave. When I find it convenient, I will send for you." At the same time he was hoping that Paul would offer him a bribe, so he sent for him frequently and talked with him.**
When two years had passed, Felix was succeeded by Porcius Festus, but because Felix wanted to grant a favor to the Jews, he left Paul in prison.

But the chief priests and Jewish leaders wanted to have Paul transferred to Jerusalem, for they were preparing an ambush to kill Paul.

■ **Memory Verse:**
II Timothy 2:3
Endure hardship with us like a good soldier of Christ Jesus.

■ **Character Trait:**
Confidence—a feeling of security based on faith and trust. It is the firm belief that God can see you safely through all of life's problems.

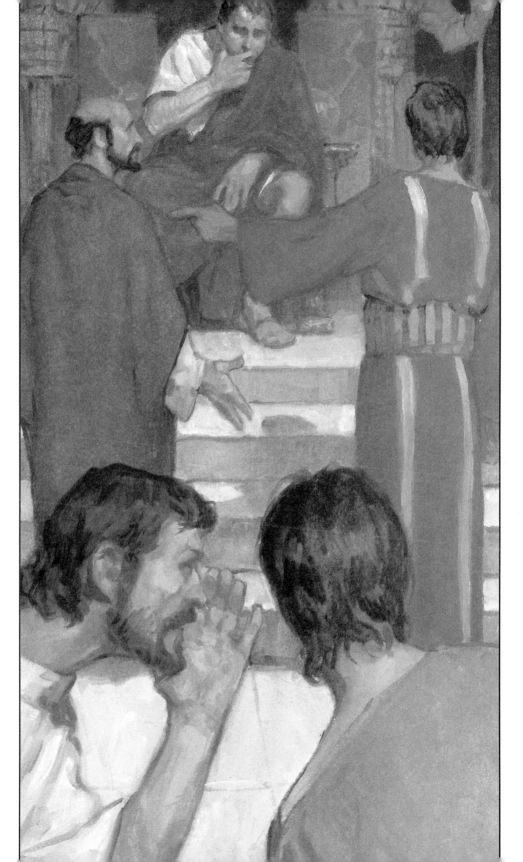

A Gripping Defense

After two years in prison, Paul appeared before Festus, the Roman governor, and demanded his right to be tried by Emperor Nero at Rome. But first, Festus brought Paul before King Agrippa, who was visiting the city. With King Agrippa's permission, Paul preached to him.

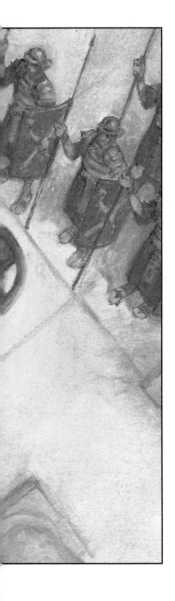

📖 **Then Agrippa said to Paul, "Do you think that in such a short time you can persuade me to be a Christian?"**

Paul replied, "Short time or long— I pray God that not only you but all who are listening to me today may become what I am, except for these chains."

The king rose, and with him the governor and Bernice and those sitting with them. They left the room, and while talking with one another, they said, "This man is not doing anything that deserves death or imprisonment."

Agrippa said to Festus, "This man could have been set free if he had not appealed to Caesar."

Paul was sent to Rome to appeal to Caesar.

■ Memory Verse:
I Peter 3:15b
Always be prepared to give an answer to everyone who asks you to give the reason for the hope that you have. But do this with gentleness and respect.

■ Character Trait:
Repentance—sorrow for one's sin and turning away from that sin to serve God and do right. Repentance involves admitting to God that you did something wrong, feeling sorry for that wrongdoing, and changing your behavior from wrong actions to right ones.

Rough Sailing

Festus handed Paul over to a centurion named Julius, who admired Paul. They sailed for Rome. A violent storm attacked the ship. But Paul encouraged the crew.

📖 **But now I urge you to keep up your courage, because not one of you will be lost; only the ship will be destroyed. Last night an angel of the God whose I am and whom I**

serve stood beside me and said, "Do not be afraid, Paul. You must stand trial before Caesar; and God has graciously given you the lives of all who sail with you." So keep up your courage, men, for I have faith in God that it will happen just as he told me. Nevertheless, we must run aground on some island.

The storm raged on. On the fourteenth day, land was spotted. Eventually, the ship ran aground and broke apart.

 The soldiers planned to kill the prisoners to prevent any of them from swimming away and escaping. But the centurion wanted to spare Paul's life and kept them from carrying out their plan. He ordered those who could swim to jump overboard first and get to land. The rest were to get there on planks or on pieces of the ship. In this way everyone reached land in safety.

Paul's prediction of everyone arriving on land safely had come true.

■ Memory Verse:
Psalm 55:22
Cast your cares on the Lord and he will sustain you; he will never let the righteous fall.

■ Character Trait:
Kindness—combines a sympathetic attitude with the willingness to be helpful whenever possible. Kindness begins with consideration for others and is demonstrated when specific needs arise. Julius, a kind centurion who wanted to spare Paul's life, did not let the soldiers kill the prisoners.

Trust the Word

Near the end of his life Paul was imprisoned in a dark, cold dungeon in Rome. While there he wrote two letters to his friend Timothy. He encouraged Timothy to be faithful to God.

📖 **But as for you, continue in what you have learned and have become convinced of, because you know those from whom you learned it, and how from infancy you have known the holy Scriptures, which are able to make you wise for salvation through faith in Christ Jesus. All Scripture is God-breathed and is useful for teaching, rebuking, correcting and training in righteousness, so that the man of God may be thoroughly equipped for every good work.**
In the presence of God and of Christ Jesus, who will judge the living and the dead, and in view of his appearing and his kingdom, I give you this charge: Preach the Word; be prepared in season and out of season; correct, rebuke and encourage— with great patience and careful instruction.

Paul warned Timothy that men would not always welcome the Gospel, and told him to keep his head, endure hardship, and do the work of an evangelist.

■ Memory Verse:

II Timothy 3:16
All Scripture is God-breathed and is useful for teaching, rebuking, correcting and training in righteousness.

■ Character Trait:

Commitment—a willingness to serve someone or a cause. It involves your mental and physical loyalties to that person or purpose. A commitment should be taken seriously, especially where your relationship with God is concerned. Paul was committed to preaching the Gospel, and died for his faith. He wanted Timothy to have a strong commitment to preach even if others wanted to harm him because of it.

Freedom in Forgiveness

Onesimus was a runaway slave. He belonged to a man named Philemon, who was a Christian and a friend of Paul. If a runaway slave was caught, he could be killed. Paul wrote a letter to Philemon asking him to have mercy on Onesimus, who had served Paul while Paul was in prison.

📖 **So if you consider me a partner, welcome him as you would welcome me. If he has done you any wrong or owes you anything, charge it to me. I, Paul, am writing this with my own hand. I will pay it back—not to mention that you owe me your very self. I do wish, brother, that I may have some benefit from you in the Lord; refresh my heart in Christ. Confident of your obedience, I write to you, knowing that you will do even more than I ask.**

Paul was so confident that his friend Philemon would do as he asked, that he asked Philemon to prepare a room for his visit.

■ Memory Verse:

Ephesians 4:32
Be kind and compassionate to one another, forgiving each other, just as in Christ God forgave you.

■ Character Trait:

Forgiveness—forgetting or blotting out someone's sin or guilt. Any request for forgiveness should go with a desire to make up for the wrong. The slave Onesimus had asked Jesus to forgive his sins. Now he needed to ask Philemon to forgive him for the wrong he had done. Philemon needed to forgive Onesimus.

A Grown Man Grows Up

Though Peter was one of Jesus' disciples, he didn't start out as a giant in his faith. He needed to grow in Christ. Growth didn't happen right away. Peter wrote letters to Christians in the early church to describe what he had learned about growing spiritually.

📖 **His divine power has given us everything we need for life and godliness through our knowledge of him who called us by his own glory and goodness. Through these he has given us his very great and precious promises, so that through them you may participate in the divine nature and escape the corruption in the world caused by evil desires.**
For this very reason, make every effort to add to your faith goodness; and to goodness, knowledge; and to knowledge, self-control; and to self-control, perseverance; and to perseverance, godliness; and to godliness, brotherly kindness; and to brotherly kindness, love. For if you possess these qualities in increasing measure, they will keep you from being ineffective and unproductive in your knowledge of our Lord Jesus Christ. But if anyone does not have them, he is nearsighted and blind, and has forgotten that he has been cleansed from his past sins.
Therefore, my brothers, be all the more eager to make your calling and election sure. For if you do these things, you will never fall, and you will receive a rich welcome into the eternal kingdom of our Lord and Savior Jesus Christ.

Peter knew he was going to die soon, and he might not get another chance to remind his friends of these things.

■ Memory Verse:
Philippians 1:6b
Being confident of this, that he who began a good work in you will carry it on to completion until the day of Christ Jesus.

■ Character Trait:
Dedication—complete commitment to something or someone. When you are dedicated, your whole heart is in what you are doing. Dedication may involve the setting apart of something or someone for a special purpose.

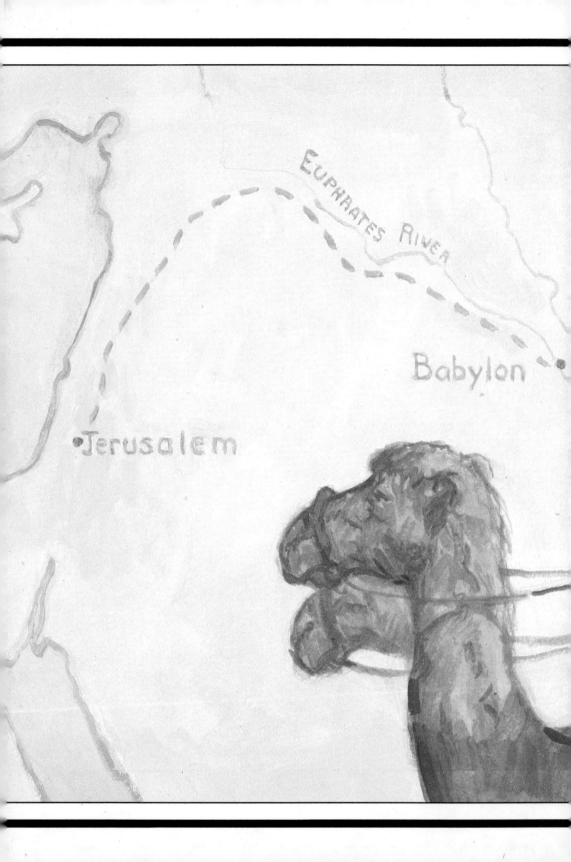